Reluctant Heroes

Reluctant Heroes

True Five-Minute-Read Adventure Stories for Boys

Kendall Haven

LIBRARIES UNLIMITED

A Member of the Greenwood Publishing Group

Westport, Connecticut • London

Library of Congress Cataloging-in-Publication Data

Haven, Kendall F.
  Reluctant heroes : true five-minute-read adventure stories for boys / Kendall Haven.
    p. cm.
  Includes bibliographical references and index.
  ISBN 978-1-59158-749-1 (alk. paper)
  1. Heroes—Biography. 2. Courage. 3. Storytelling. I. Title.
  CT104.H38 2008
  920.02—dc22   2008014017

British Library Cataloguing in Publication Data is available.

Library of Congress Catalog Card Number: 2008014017
ISBN: 978-1-59158-749-1

First published in 2008

Libraries Unlimited, 88 Post Road West, Westport, CT 06881
A Member of the Greenwood Publishing Group, Inc.
www.lu.com

Printed in the United States of America

The paper used in this book complies with the
Permanent Paper Standard issued by the National
Information Standards Organization (Z39.48–1984).

10 9 8 7 6 5 4 3 2 1

To Sharon Coatney, who created the idea for this book and has guided and inspired many of my recent projects.

Contents

STORIES FROM MODERN LIFE ❧ 69

Introduction

Few people think of themselves as heroes or feel like heroes. Few believe that they have done anything heroic. Heroic acts always feel like the amazing things that somebody else does. Yet heroes—ordinary heroes, reluctant heroes—are all around us—in your school, in your neighborhood, likely even in your own house!

The dictionary provides two primary definitions for the word *hero*. First, in myth: a hero is a man of great strength and courage who is favored by the gods. Hmmmm. That doesn't sound like us. That's the kind of hero that is always someone famous and with rippled and bulging muscles. Movies are made about that kind of hero. That kind of hero lives in the glamorous spotlight.

Now look at the second, more general definition of hero. The dictionary says that a hero is "any person admired for courage, nobility, or exploits."

This is the *real* definition of a hero—someone who acts with courage and nobility. This is how ordinary people rise up to become heroes. They act. They do things that require real courage, things that are noble. Heroes do what is right—even when it requires much effort and involves great risks and dangers. Do *those* things and others will notice and will admire you for it. Presto! You have become a hero.

Most heroes, however, didn't set out to be heroes. They didn't want to face danger and struggle. Usually, they had to be dragged—forced—to act heroically. Mostly people we call heroes think of themselves as just ordinary people.

But these Reluctant Heroes are the best models for the rest of us. They represent our highest ideal, our greatest potential. We all have the ability to rise up to heroic greatness when the opportunity arises. We all possess the "right stuff." There is no need to wait for great moments in history. Suitable opportunities for heroism abound.

The catch is that they come loaded with fear, with dread, with struggles, with danger, with the probability of failure and embarrassment. Yet, that is exactly what makes those moments opportunities for our own heroics. Face the danger. Risk the failure, the ridicule, and the consequences. That is the stuff of true Reluctant Heroes.

Here are 25 stories of Reluctant Heroes. They are all ordinary beings on our planet. None asked for the opportunity to act heroically. None wanted it. Yet, in their own way, they each accepted the yoke once it was thrust in front of them. They acted. They did what they had to do. They didn't sidestep the danger and give up.

Thus, they and their stories are empowering and inspiring models for us all. We are all reluctant to become even momentary heroes. None want to leave the safety and comfort of the sidelines. Yet each time you do, you have the opportunity to become a true hero—a Reluctant Hero. Each of us crouches in waiting, mostly hoping to be passed over and not have to shoulder the mantle of hero. Yet opportunities come to us all.

Try this. Award yourself the title of *Reluctant Hero* first. Try it on. See how it feels. It may help you be ready to face the risk and dangers every heroic act includes. When we step up to heroically face danger, risk, and struggle for a noble cause, we become the heroes for everyone else. Your heroics lift other people's vision, their image of the possible, their sense of hope and optimism. What could be more powerful or empowering than to be surrounded by Reluctant Heroes?

I hope you enjoy these 25 stories and these Reluctant Heroes. Then find your own stories of Reluctant Heroes ... or create your own!

Using This Book

The stories in this book are short (five-minute reads), true, high-adventure stories. Five are new stories that have not been published. Twenty are shortened versions of stories I have previously published (coming from seven different collections of themed stories). I refer you to the listed source books for the complete stories and highly recommend that you see those source books to find additional background material and follow-up questions and activities as well as the complete stories.

All 25 of the stories in this book depict true (nonfiction) events. These are stories that have really happened as presented here. Where any aspect of a story has been created or inferred from available records and research (such as dialogue), I have so noted in the About This Story sections. That will let you determine exactly what is reliably accurate and what is only typical or probably accurate.

The stories in this book are divided into three groupings: stories from history, stories from modern life, and stories from nature. Historical stories are organized chronologically.

Each story includes two additional sections. The About This Story section presents a brief overview of the story, providing perspective information so that the reader may place this story within an overall context. This section also includes some background information on the events and characters described in the story. The For Further Reading section presents a limited number of book references to allow readers to extend their interest in the central topics and themes of each story into other works.

Because these stories are nonfiction, they can be linked with school curriculum units and can be used to teach as well as to inspire and entertain. They demonstrate the structure and architecture of effective stories as well as provide engrossing and memorable moments and role models for students who listen to or read them.

Stories from History

Staring into the Whites of Their Eyes
The Battle of Bunker Hill: June 17, 1775

This story is extracted with publisher's permission from a story of the same name in *Voices of the American Revolution* (Libraries Unlimited, 2000). See *Voices of the American Revolution* for the complete story and for additional references and follow-up activities.

ABOUT THIS STORY

Following the battles of Lexington and Concord, over 20,000 citizen soldiers armed with muskets and clubs poured into a great ring surrounding the British forces in Boston.

Trapped in Boston were 5,000 British soldiers protected by the mighty guns of the British fleet anchored in the harbor. However, massed artillery on high ground either north or south of Boston could control the city. Those heights to the north, on Charlestown peninsula, were named Bunker Hill (the taller of the two hills) and Breed's Hill (the hill closer to Boston).

During the night of Friday, June 17, 1775, rebel forces moved to occupy Breed's Hill and to dig an earthen fort where they could install cannon to fire into Boston. Saturday morning the British Navy bombarded the half-dug fort. Early that afternoon British ground forces (redcoats) attacked.

Just imagine how terrifying that British attack would have felt to a boy crouching in the American trenches. But that is exactly what happened to 12-year-old Robert Ballard, who snuck up the hill during the night and joined in the effort to dig the fort. The characters and events in this story are historically accurate. The specific dialogue is fiction but based on available historic records.

Staring into the Whites of Their Eyes

At 12:30 a lookout down the line cried, "They're coming!" Over 40 long transport boats shoved off from Boston piers in neat precision. Two thousand five hundred hardened redcoats sat in orderly rows. Eight hundred oars flashed in the sunlight and dipped in unison into the calm blue waters of Boston Bay. Rank after red rank off-loaded on the beach to form a sea of red coats and white breeches and a forest of gleaming bayonets.

Patriot couriers on horseback raced from point to point, exchanging news and battle plans, making requests, offering aid. But 12-year-old Robert Ballard noticed none of it. He saw only the sea of dragon-fire red that was intent on killing every man in this pitiful excuse for an earthen fort. He heard only the pounding drums and shrill English fifes. He stared only at the rows of snapping banners announcing that doom had arrived for the foolish rabble on the hill.

Suddenly Robert felt like a helpless little boy snared in a deadly man's world. This was no game, and he suddenly knew that he did not belong here.

"Dig!" growled the man next to Robert. Mechanically, he returned to his shoveling as a hot sun beat down overhead, cannon balls screeched past, and the terror of the pounding drums beat deep in his soul.

"Here they come!" cried a lookout, and the endless red lines, that unstoppable English war machine, a glittering host of red, white, gold, and steel, advanced steadily up the unmowed grass of Breed's Hill to slaughter any fool who stood in their path.

The ground vibrated with the tramping of their countless feet. The air was shattered by the dreadful noise of their drums. With all the pomp and ceremony of a royal wedding, death marched toward the rebel lines.

Shovels were cast aside. Muskets were hurriedly loaded. A tense hush fell over the fresh-dug fort.

With no musket, Robert clutched his shovel and pressed into the cool fresh-smelling dirt. General Israel Putnam ("Old Put") galloped along the trench line of waiting volunteers crying, "Hold your fire, lads! Don't fire till you see the whites of their eyes."

An eerie silence fell upon the hill as the distance closed between defenders and redcoats. Robert glanced over the dirt wall and all before him was a sea of deadly red and gleaming steel.

Only 400 feet separated the armies. Now 300 feet; now 250. Robert could scarcely breathe with the tension that lay so thick and heavy upon him.

Someone yelled, "Fire!" Flame and smoke erupted from Patriot muskets. The British ranks melted. Their stiff lines disintegrated as if mowed by a heavenly scythe. It seemed a solid sheet of flame and a wall of raging musket balls ripped across the deadly open space as Patriot musketeers feverishly reloaded to pour round after round into the grim sea of attackers.

The gleaming British ranks staggered and faltered. Their momentum turned to liquid red flowing out to stain the grass. Like a spent wave, the British ranks stumbled back into retreat.

Cheers erupted all along the Patriot line. Hats were tossed in the air. Jeers were tossed down the hill.

Robert opened his eyes and raised his head. A euphoric wave of relief swept over him. A feeling of power and glory surged through his body. He shouted, "We won! We won!"

"Wait. Here they come again," called someone down the line. Red ranks had reformed at the bottom of Breed's Hill. Again the drums pounded. Again the rows of British cannon spit fire and screaming shells at the fort. The mighty red war engine rewound for another push up the deadly slope.

"Reload!" cried Col. Prescott. The man next to Robert muttered that he was low on ammo. So was everyone else.

Col. Prescott hauled Robert up by his collar and pointed toward the milling units standing idle at the base and rear of Bunker Hill. "Boy, we need reinforcements and more ammo! Get those units up here! Go!"

Robert tore like the wind across the ragged dirt of the fort and down the back slope of Breed's Hill. Group after group refused. At the safe base of the hill they and their ammo sat, and there they would stay.

Then Breed's Hill erupted in fire again. The thunder of a thousand muskets tore through the air. Robert sped back up the slope, arriving just as a mighty cheer roared down the Patriot line. "They're falling back again!" Hats flew. Flags were waved from behind the fence and walls.

The dense sulfur smoke of gunpowder made Robert choke as he scrambled back into his spot in the trench. But he couldn't make himself jump and cheer with the others. He could see a dozen Patriots sprawled dead in the soft dirt. Many more groaned with the agony of wounds as comrades offered aid. Two of the dead were men Robert had spoken to earlier that day. One had shown him how to hold his shovel so as to not get blisters.

Then he gazed over the wall—and felt sick. The slope was littered with hundreds of fallen redcoats. Some tried to crawl. The screams of wounded filled the air. Most lay as crumpled lumps on the field. The trampled grass was coated thick and slick with blood. So many dead who, an hour ago, laughed and chatted with friends, who, an hour ago, had wives and families.

Robert sank to his knees, gasping to catch his breath, head spinning with the awful vision of that sloping field. At least the terrible fight was over and they could go home. At least they had won.

"Here they come again!" cried several lookouts on the wall. Cries of "Ammo!" "Ammo!" echoed up and down the line. "Who's got ammo?" The man next to Robert stared blankly at his empty musket. "How can I drive them off without any powder cartridges and musket balls?"

Col. Prescott snatched Robert up by the collar. "Where are the reinforcements, boy? Where's the ammo?"

Tears flowed through Robert's eyes. "They wouldn't come, sir. I told them but they wouldn't come."

Prescott cursed and turned away. Then he breathed deep and sprang to the top of the wall. "Hold back until they're right on top of us, lads. Make every shot count!"

He jumped down just as British musket balls began to thud into the dirt wall and to whine overhead. A farmer, turned volunteer soldier, sagged backward with a surprised yelp when he edged too high and a British musket ball abruptly ended his life. Robert snatched the farmer's loaded musket and cradled it to his chest as he trembled in the trench.

"Steady, boys.... Steady ..."

Robert sneaked one eye up for a peek and stared into the very face of the oncoming British. Grim faces, red coats, and gleaming steel were upon them.

"Steady ..."

They seemed no more than five long paces away, their faces as clear as the men around him in the trench.

"Steady ..."

"Fire!"

For a third time, a sheet of flame and musket ball exploded from the fort. For a third time the British line staggered and faltered as a new crop of dead sprawled to the ground.

But the wall of Patriot fire could not continue as before. As soon as it had started, the Patriot fire dimmed from ferocious roar to an occasional pop, and then fell silent. Their ammo was gone.

The redcoats charged. Men on both sides of Robert fell dead from a British volley as the first wave stormed over the wall. Robert pointed his musket at the surging red tide and squeezed the trigger. Fire and smoke belched from its mouth. The musket recoiled, twisting out of Robert's hands. He screamed and fled, sprinting like a jackrabbit away from the terror on Breed's Hill, one tiny dot in the stream of fleeing Patriot defenders.

FOR FURTHER READING

Here are a few good books to let you read more about the Battle of Bunker Hill and the early days of the Revolutionary War.

Bacon, Paul, ed. *The Uncommon Soldier of the Revolution.* Harrisburg, PA: Eastern Acorn Press, 1986.

Englar, M. *The Battle of Bunker Hill.* Mankato, MN: Compass Point Books, 2007.

Fleming, T. *Liberty: The American Revolution.* New York: Viking, 1997.

Haven, K. *Voices of the American Revolution.* Westport, CT: Libraries Unlimited, 2000.

Ingram, S. *Triangle Histories of the Revolutionary War: Battle of Bunker Hill.* Chicago: Blackbirch Press, 2003.

Ketchum, R. *Decisive Day: The Battle for Bunker Hill.* New York: Owl Books, 1999.

Kriby, P., and J. Edens. *Glorious Day, Dreadful Day: The Battle of Bunker Hill.* New York: Steck-Vaughn, 1992.

Parker, F. *Colonel William Prescott: The Commander in the Battle of Bunker Hill.* New York: Kessinger, 2007.

See your librarian for additional titles.

Children Choose
Friends Torn Apart by Political Loyalties, September 1776

This story is extracted with publisher's permission from a story of the same name in *Voices of the American Revolution* (Libraries Unlimited, 2000). See *Voices of the American Revolution* for the complete story and for additional references and follow-up activities.

ABOUT THIS STORY

A small but passionate and vocal minority of colonists actively favored independence. Approximately an equal number adamantly opposed independence. The vast majority lay in the middle. They felt loyalty to both sides, but did not passionately support either. They had always been both British citizens and Americans. How could they pick between country and mother?

But choose they had to. That was where the real revolution occurred—in the minds and hearts of ordinary American citizens. In many respects, the "real war" wasn't fought on battlefields, but in small towns across the continent. This war was fought not with soldiers, but between ordinary citizens who had to wrestle inside their own conscience and then in the public square of their town against and with their loved and trusted neighbors.

Living in the town of Poughkeepsie, New York, 10-year-old Rebecca Vandermeer and 11-year-old Jeremy Schlister had been friends since early childhood. His father was committed to the revolution and had joined the local Committee of Safety. Mr. Vandermeer was a wealthy merchant and a leader in the local Tory (loyalist) movement. After the Declaration of Independence was published (July 1776), local tensions increased. Both sets of parents ordered their children to stop playing with anyone who supported the other side.

The characters and events in this story are historically accurate. The specific dialogue is fiction but based on available historic records.

Children Choose

After school on a warm September afternoon, 1776, Jeremy Schlister and Rebecca Vandermeer lingered in the empty lot behind the school before Jeremy had to head home to finish his farm chores.

"I'll help," Rebecca offered. "I like your farm."

Jeremy hesitated. "You better not. If my father caught you out there …"

Both children paused and cocked their heads as the sound of a rumbling commotion back near the center of town drifted toward the schoolyard. They raced to see what was afoot and found a thick crowd packed onto Williams Street blocking their view. Nearer the center they could hear shouting—angry, vicious, and mean.

The thunderclap of a musket shot made the crowd gasp and squeal. Screams rose from the center along with frantic shouts and threats. Ducking, crawling, wiggling, Rebecca and Jeremy threaded their way to the inside.

Two packs of angry men faced each other on the street like miniature armies on a battlefield. Bricks, knives, and clubs were held high in the air. Several held muskets. One of them was still smoking.

"He was going to throw that knife at me, I swear it," stammered the man holding the smoking musket.

"You've killed him!" hissed a man cradling the head and shoulders of a man lying over a growing pool of his own blood.

Rebecca stood, rooted to the rut-filled road, and stared wide-eyed at the blood. She could scarcely make herself breathe. Jeremy stared at the man holding the smoking gun. It was his father's cousin.

"I swear. It was self-defense."

A uniformed constable arrived, blowing frantically on his whistle, and muscled his way through the crowd. "What's all this now?" he demanded, trying to restore calm and order.

Mr. Vandermeer, standing beside the fallen man, shook an angry finger at the opposing mob of men. His voice squeaked out high and tight. "Those ... thugs of the rebel Committee of Safety started this—pushing and shoving elderly Mr. Balkner just because he properly supports the king and Parliament. We came to his defense and tried to break it up ..."

"This town will be better off when the likes of you are run out on a rail!" shouted someone. All the men on the rebel side growled their agreement.

The constable raised his hands and scowled in turn at both mobs of men. "Order! Order! I will have order here! This is not a war ..."

"Yes, it is," shouted one of the rebels, shaking a copy of the Declaration of Independence in his clenched fist. "A war for our liberty!"

"Not here it's not!" shouted the constable. "There's no war in Poughkeepsie. Let's be civil and put down the weapons."

There followed much grumbling from both sides and painfully slow compliance as those in the front rows lowered guns, resheathed knives, and dropped bricks, clubs, and stones.

Rebecca's heart pounded at the deadly tension of this drama. It terrified her to see adults from her very own community turn on each other like savage animals. She felt that every shred of safety had been stripped away and that Poughkeepsie had turned into a wild jungle.

A heavy brick sailed from the back of the rebel side and struck Mr. Vandermeer over his left eye. He collapsed to the street. Thick streams of blood flowed across his face and hair to mix with the dust of Williams Street.

Rebecca screamed and, still clutching Jeremy's hand, raced to her father.

A shot rang out from a rooftop and the rebel who had thrown the brick spun like a scarecrow and dropped to the street.

Again the mob froze.

"Cease this firing!" screamed the constable as a police squad of reinforcements raced in, each blowing their shrill whistles, cheeks puffed out, and elbowed through the crowd.

Jeremy's father saw him still standing with Rebecca as she knelt, trembling, next to her father. "Get over here, boy. What are you doin' on the stinkin' Tories' side?"

Embarrassed at suddenly being the center of attention, Jeremy dropped his head and scurried to his father. Mr. Schlister whapped Jeremy's ear hard with his open hand. "I tole you not to play with her no more, boy!" Mr. Schlister actually lifted Jeremy off the ground by his shoulders and shook him violently like a rag doll before slamming him back down.

"But father …" Jeremy began. Whap! Mr. Schlister's fist slammed into the side of his son's head, making Jeremy's knees wobble.

The crowd slowly dissipated as a line of police separated Patriot and Loyalist. Each side hurled angry taunts and threats as they retreated. An eerie calm and three pools of blood were left to mark the spot of Poughkeepsie's entry into the Revolutionary War.

Rebecca and Jeremy met the next day at school and edged cautiously toward each other.

Two older boys (with a young girl tagging along beside them) watched from across the street. One yelled at Jeremy, "Why are you talking to a *Tory?*" The other sneered, "Jeremy is a Tory.… Jeremy is a Tory."

"I am not!" Jeremy yelled back, turning beet red.

"Don't let them *taunt* you. They're just *ignorant*," Rebecca whispered.

Jeremy angrily shrank away from her. "I'm not a Tory!"

The boys swaggered across the street. The young girl followed at their heels. "Then why are you talking to *her?*"

One of the boys shoved Rebecca. She sprawled onto the grass only to bound back to her feet. "You stop that, Miles Hoffman!"

The young girl darted out from behind her brother's legs and kicked Rebecca. When Rebecca doubled over to grab her shin, the girl spit on her.

The older boys laughed. One pushed Rebecca again, hard. She crashed down, tearing her dress and grinding her face into the dirt. Almost as fast as she fell, Rebecca scrambled back to her feet, eyes filled with fury, fists clenched.

Miles Hoffman turned to Jeremy and demanded, "Should I tell everyone that you're a Tory lover, or are you going to stand up for your liberty like a man?"

All eyes turned to Jeremy as his gaze flitted from Rebecca to the boys and back. He slowly stepped to Rebecca.

She tried to hide a smile as she whispered, "Whew! For a minute I thought …"

He whispered, "Sorry," and shoved her viciously into a row of bushes along the edge of the school yard. Rebecca sprawled through the thorny hedges and tumbled across the grass.

Jeremy shouted, "I choose America!" With arms around the shoulders of older boys, he laughed and pointed at Rebecca's mud-smeared face and ruined dress as he jogged back across the road.

FOR FURTHER READING

Here are a few good books to let you read more about the civil strife that was such a big part of the Revolutionary War.

Adler, Jeanne. *In the Path of War: Children of the American Revolution Tell Their Stories*. Peterborough, NH: Cobblestone Publishing, 1998.

Bacon, Paul, ed. *The Uncommon Soldier of the Revolution*. Harrisburg, PA: Eastern Acorn Press, 1986.

Bobrick, B. *Fight for Freedom: The American Revolutionary War*. New York: Atheneum, 2004.

Fleming, T. *Liberty: The American Revolution*. New York: Viking, 1997.

Haven, K. *Voices of the American Revolution*. Westport, CT: Libraries Unlimited, 2000.

Herbert, J. *The American Revolution for Kids*. Chicago: Chicago Review Press, 2002.

Hibbert, C. *Redcoats and Rebels: The American Revolution through British Eyes*. New York: W. W. Norton, 2002.

Morris, Richard. *The American Revolution*. Minneapolis, MN: Lerner, 1995.

Murphy, J. *Young Patriot: The American Revolution Experienced by One Boy*. New York: Houghton Mifflin, 1998.

Schomp, V. *The Revolutionary War*. London: Marshall Cavendish, 2003.

See your librarian for additional titles.

Patriotic Plunder

A Cabin Boy's View of Naval Warfare during the Revolution, September 1779

This story is extracted with publisher's permission from a story of the same name in *Voices of the American Revolution* (Libraries Unlimited, 2000). See *Voices of the American Revolution* for the complete story and for additional references and follow-up activities.

ABOUT THIS STORY

America had no navy when the Revolutionary War erupted—only fishing boats and a few small merchant cargo vessels. Neither was there a national treasury nor budget to build ships. Still, the war could not be won without somehow challenging England's dominion on the open seas. So Congress authorized individuals, cities, and states to build and arm their own ships to attack British interests. These ships acted like pirates but, because they were sanctioned by Congress, they were officially called "privateers."

Many privateer ships were sunk or captured. But many gathered huge profits for their crew. All of them harassed British shipping and diminished British ability to supply their army fighting on American soil.

Israel Trask was 12 when he was hired on as cabin boy to the American privateer two-masted schooner *Black Prince*. When he climbed on board in May 1779, it was the first time he had set foot on any ship bigger than a row boat. The story of Israel Trask shows the typical life of privateers and also includes the story of the greatest American naval disaster of the war.

The characters and events in this story are historically accurate. The specific dialogue is fiction but based on available historic records.

Patriotic Plunder

In mid-September, the *Black Prince* was set to sail from Portsmouth. Cookie looked worried as the *Black Prince* slipped out of Portsmouth harbor. "What's wrong, Cookie?" asked Israel.

"Owner signed us on to attack a British fort."

"Just us?" gulped Israel.

"Nay, lad. We're joinin' a flotilla. Owner signed an agreement with Congress to have us join with 18 privateers, three Navy ships, and over 20 transports to attack a fort the British are building on the high bluffs overlooking the mouth of the Penobscot River [along the southern coast of what is now Maine]. You mark my words, lad, this voyage will be all trouble and no money."

In two days the *Black Prince* joined the flotilla just as it rounded a rocky point in high winds and choppy seas and came within sight of the fort—barely two walls built, but already a row of cannons mounted and ready to fire. Six British Navy frigates lay at anchor in the harbor.

The ship's bell clanged. The captain's whistle blew. "All hands on deck! Battle stations!"

Two American Navy warships led the attack: the *Warren* and the *Hazard*. Cannons roared from 14 of the attacking ships. Answering cannons belched fire and smoke from the fort and the British ships. Seawater exploded around the *Black Prince*. One mast on the *Warren* was hit and toppled to the deck. Cannon balls shrieked through the air thick as hail.

Israel was terrified and fascinated at the same time. He wanted to hide but couldn't tear himself away from the rail, needing to watch every shot of this mighty battle. Clouds of stinging gray smoke covered the bay.

One of the British ships exploded when a cannon ball struck a row of powder kegs. Flames and black smoke billowed into the sky. Gunners on the *Black Prince* cheered, claiming credit for the shot.

But five of the American ships had also been badly damaged. The attack was called off. The ships retreated just out of range of the fort's deadly cannons.

"This is as ugly as a situation can get," sighed Cookie. "We can't attack the fort until those ships are driven off or sunk, and we can't attack the ships until the fort is silenced."

As Israel and Cookie chopped dried potatoes and stringy beef in the galley, Cookie added, "Other British warships with 50 guns each—and maybe more—have got to be on their way here. If we don't strike fast or leave, I fear disaster."

The first inklings of dread and panic settled into the pit of Israel's stomach.

For three days the stalemate continued. While Israel and Cookie chopped stringy salt beef for lunch on the third day, the ship's bell began to urgently clang.

"All hands on deck! Battle stations!"

Israel's heart sank as he scrambled up the narrow stairs. Eight mammoth British warships were churning through the choppy waters of the outer bay. Three rows of giant cannon barrels bristled from each side of each ship.

"We're in for it now, lad. Those are 18 pounders—or even bigger. Over twice the size and range of our guns."

"All hands hoist the sails! Mains and tops! Rig fore and aft!"

"Aren't we going to man the cannons and fight?" asked Israel.

"Against them?" snorted Cookie. "We'd be blown apart afore we got off one broadside. No, we're running."

"Can we race past them out to sea?" called Israel.

"Not a chance," answered Jeremiah Douglas, next to Israel working to release the sheets. "They got the sea lanes blocked. We'll have to run up the river and hope they can't follow."

The American fleet raced for the curving Penobscot River as the fort's cannons opened fire from above. Fire from the British ships and fort rained down on the fleeing American fleet. Nine ships exploded and sank before they could enter the relative safety of the river. Eight more were badly damaged and had to be intentionally beached for fear of blocking the channel for the ships still behind them. All eight were set on fire to prevent the British from seizing and using them.

The *Hazard*, biggest of the American warships and lead vessel in the flotilla, grounded in mid-river channel. The schooner *Curran* tried to pass to starboard and also grounded. Other ships had to heave to and cast out anchors to keep from ramming into the stuck ships. British cannon balls from the mouth of the river could easily pick off the American ships as they sat at anchor.

The order was passed to burn the fleet to prevent the British from using any of the ships or their supplies. Black columns of smoke curled into the afternoon sky as the constant rumble of British cannons and the screeching of British cannon balls filled the air.

A cannon ball smashed into the side of the *Black Prince*, splintered the hull and deck timbers, and struck the store of powder kegs in the hold. The entire ship was lifted out of the water by the explosion of those kegs. It settled back into the river in a giant fireball with the hiss of steam as water poured through gaping holes in the hull.

Israel staggered to his feet in the galley as water swirled around his knees. Cookie was dead, killed in the explosion. Smoke, fire, gurgling black water, and the screams of burning and wounded men were everywhere.

The stairs had been torn away by the blast. Israel was trapped as the ship rolled heavily to port and settled lower in the river. He sucked in three deep breaths and dove under the rising water, kicking and feeling his way toward the hull. The dim light of day filtered through the river water and guided him to a monstrous hole in the belly of his dying ship. Israel kicked through and broke back into daylight as burning timbers dropped like confetti all around him.

He swam to shore and struggled up onto the bank next to three other shivering sailors from different ships. Then they turned and sprinted into the woods, seeing long lines of redcoats marching up both shores of the river to capture any survivors.

Israel walked almost 200 miles to reach home. The last hundred he managed barefoot after his shoes wore out. Yet with each step Israel Trask was dreaming of his next ship and of their next haul of plunder.

FOR FURTHER READING

Here are a few good books to let you read more about America's privateer navy and the naval aspects of the Revolutionary War.

Adler, J. *In the Path of War: Children of the American Revolution Tell Their Stories.* Peterborough, NH: Cobblestone Publishing, 1998.

Bowling, T. *Pirates and Privateers.* London: Pocket Essentials, 2008.

Fleming, T. *Liberty: The American Revolution.* New York: Viking, 1997.

Haven, K. *Voices of the American Revolution.* Westport, CT: Libraries Unlimited, 2000.

Maclay, E. *A History of American Privateers.* New York: Kessinger Publishing, 2004.

Morris, Richard. *The American Revolution.* Minneapolis, MN: Lerner, 1995.

Patton, R. *Patriot Pirates: The Privateer War for Freedom and Fortune.* New York: Pantheon, 2008.

See your librarian for additional titles.

Pigtail Spy
A Teenage Rider in the Revolutionary War
American Spy Network, February 1781

This story is extracted with publisher's permission from a story
of the same name in *Voices of the American Revolution*
(Libraries Unlimited, 2000). See *Voices of the American
Revolution* for the complete story and for additional
references and follow-up activities.

ABOUT THIS STORY

We often forget that brave Americans spied on the British
forces from South Carolina to Maine and boldly rode out
through the night to spread the word of impending British
movements.

Surprisingly, many of these spies and riders were women.
More surprisingly, many were *young* women, girls really.
Some were actual spies; some rode messenger routes to warn
local militia of British movement. A select few did both.
One of this group of unheralded fighters for American liberty
was Betsy Drowdy, who had just turned 15 in February 1781,
when General Charles Cornwallis and his British army lumbered into Hillsboro, North Carolina, to establish winter

camp. Betsy was able to get a job working for an army adjutant, Col. Fitsgerald.

On February 21, 1781, Col. Fitsgerald shared information with Betsy of a replacement cavalry column moving north from South Carolina—important information Betsy was determined to place in the hands of Col. "Light Horse" Harry Lee's Continental cavalry. This is the story of her attempt to deliver that message.

The characters and events in this story are historically accurate. The specific dialogue is fiction but based on available historic records.

Pigtail Spy

Betsy felt that she would burst before she made it home that evening. It felt that the whole revolution suddenly depended on her, alone. She had to clamp her mouth shut to keep from screaming.

This was BIG. This news could affect the whole war, and she was the only one who knew. Patriot units *had* to prevent those South Carolina Tories from joining Cornwallis!

Her parents begged her not to go. Col. "Light Horse" Harry Lee's Continental cavalry were off somewhere to the west. But no one in Hillsboro knew where. It could take days to find them and the roads teemed with British and Tory patrols.

Betsy heard not a word.

A light mist fell from a solid cover of clouds and a blustery winter wind rattled through the bare tree limbs as Betsy wrapped herself in her heavy cape and stepped from the warmth and light of the house into the dangerous dark. Silently she climbed into the saddle and leaned low as if to hide while her father's horse trotted into the night.

Betsy skirted south, wide around Hillsboro to avoid Tory patrols, before she turned west into unfamiliar territory. If she rode far enough west, she felt sure she would meet a Patriot patrol or guard post.

An hour into her trek, she heard a twig snap to her left ... or was it just the wind? No! There was another. In a blink she was surrounded by four riders with pistols drawn and aimed at her.

The riders leered as they slowly circled, firing questions at her. Who was she? Why was she on this road at night? Why should they let her pass their road block? What was a girl doing out alone?

At first Betsy was so frightened she couldn't answer and stared back helplessly, her mouth flopping open and closed.

The Tory soldiers made her dismount. They searched her horse, saddle bags, and saddle. They pried into her pockets and felt through the lining of her cape.

Finally, Betsy regained enough composure to say, "I work for Col. Fitsgerald, General Cornwallis' adjutant. He has given me permission for this ride."

"Sorry," said the patrol leader, showing sudden respect for Betsy, "but *no one* is permitted to pass to the west of this post. You'll have to turn back."

Not knowing what else to do, Betsy turned her horse around and started back toward Hillsboro. But it never occurred to her to give up. After several hundred yards, she thought she could see a wide field through the deep gloom that stretched out to the south side of the road. She spurred her horse into a full gallop as she turned into the field.

"Get her!" cried a voice. A shot rang out. Then another.

Betsy jabbed her heels into her horse's flanks and sped through the black night across the field. Distant hoof beats told her she was being chased by the patrol. Occasional thunder-clap shots and flashes of fire told her they were not very far behind.

Through the field. Across a low wall. Through a small pasture. Over a fence. Into a thick and tangled woods she rode. Branches and tree trunks forced her to slow to a fast trot to keep from being knocked off her horse. Even then she rode with one arm up to protect her face. Her cape was torn off. Branches, vines, and bramble shredded her skirt. The dense woods seemed to last forever as she blindly stumbled forward, terrified that at any moment one of the Tory riders would reach out from the dark and grab her.

Groping her way past trees and vines, Betsy veered her horse to the right around a thick cluster of trees and stumbled into a deep ravine. Dizzy and stunned, she stopped at the bottom and dismounted. Holding her horse's muzzle to keep it from snorting or braying, she tried to hold her own breath so she could listen for the Tory riders.

At first she only heard the pounding of her own heart. Then, faintly at first, she heard the snapping and crackling of breaking branches. They were coming, following her trail. "Through here," called a voice, growing ever closer.

Now Betsy could hear the heavy breathing of horses. Now she could hear branches scraping across leather leggings of the riders. Now she could hear the breathing of the men.

"Spread out a little. Look for broken branches or bits of cloth," called one voice that seemed to come from right on top of her.

"I know what to do, and if'n you'd hush up, Billy, I'd see if'n I can hear her up ahead," whined another.

"We shouldn't leave our guard post this long," said a third, sounding like he had already passed Betsy's hiding spot. "What if the captain comes by?"

Slowly the voices and stomping of hooves faded into the night. Betsy was alone again. For almost an hour she was too terrified to move. Had they stopped? Were they waiting for her?

But she had to push on and find Col. Lee's Continental cavalry.

Except now she was lost. She had no idea of how far she had ridden or in what direction. She had no idea which way was west. She was as likely to ride right back into the Tory lines as to escape to find the Continentals.

Betsy sucked in a deep, slow breath to calm herself and led her horse back to the top of the ravine. She mounted, wished for luck, and turned her horse in the direction that felt most like west.

The ground grew softer. Pools of standing water suddenly seemed to lie in every direction. She had stumbled into a swamp!

The horse balked and whinnied. Betsy patted its neck and urged it forward. Gingerly it eased through the muck and mud. Hanging tendrils of Spanish moss brushed across Betsy's face. It felt like snakes sliding down her skin.

There was a loud splash off to her left. The horse bucked and reared. Betsy was thrown off, splattering into knee-deep water, mud, and cattails. By the time she scrambled to her feet, the horse was gone.

The swamp and the night closed upon Betsy like a smothering blanket. She was lost, alone, and on foot in a pitch-black swamp. She would have hidden if there had been anywhere to hide. She would have cried out if she thought anyone was there to hear.

Instead she did the only thing she could think of to do. She began to walk and wade through the ooze and slime of the swamp. On every step she was sure a snake was waiting to bite her or an alligator was about to clamp onto her leg.

Still she walked—walked and sobbed from fright and frustration. She had failed in her attempt to reach the Continentals and would probably die in the swamp before morning.

As first light began to dull the grays of the eastern sky, Betsy scrambled onto raised ground and found a road which bordered the swamp. She looked worse than a half-drowned rat as she plopped onto the deep dirt ruts to catch her breath and quiet her choking sobs.

Almost before she sat, a man stepped from the shadows with a gun.

The man knelt and asked if he could help. He introduced himself as a sergeant in the Continental cavalry.

Betsy's sobs turned to a flood of joyful tears as she poured out her story.

FOR FURTHER READING

Here are a few good books to let you read more about American spies and message networks during the Revolutionary War.

Adler, Jeanne. *In the Path of War: Children of the American Revolution Tell Their Stories*. Peterborough, NH: Cobblestone Publishing, 1998.

Allen, T. *George Washington, Spymaster: How the Americans Outspied the British and Won the Revolutionary War*. Washington, DC: National Geographic Society, 2007.

Bacon, Paul, ed. *The Uncommon Soldier of the Revolution*. Harrisburg, PA: Eastern Acorn Press, 1986.

Bracken, J., ed. *Women in the American Revolution*. Carlisle, MA: Discovery Enterprises, Ltd., 1997.

Canon, J. *Heroines of the American Revolution*. Santa Barbara, CA: Bellerophon Books, 1994.

Greenberg, J., and H. McKeever. *In Their Own Words: Journal of a Revolutionary War Woman*. New York: Franklin Watts, 1996.

Haven, K. *Amazing American Women*. Englewood, CO: Libraries Unlimited, 1996.

———. *Voices of the American Revolution*. Westport, CT: Libraries Unlimited, 2000.

See your librarian for additional titles.

Diary of Death
The Siege of Vicksburg, May–July 1863

This story is extracted with publisher's permission from a story of the same name in *Voices of the American Civil War* (Libraries Unlimited, 2002). See *Voices of the American Civil War* for the complete story and for additional references and follow-up activities.

ABOUT THIS STORY

While the war in the east dragged on through its long series of duels between the Federal Army of the Potomac and the Confederate Army of Northern Virginia, Federal eyes turned to the war in the west—to the Mississippi River. Admiral David Farrugut steamed into the mouth of the Mississippi and began his push to conquer the river from the south in early 1862. General Ulysses S. Grant fought south along the great river with his Union army from Kentucky and Tennessee to meet Farrugut.

By late 1862, Vicksburg, the powerful citadel sitting on high bluffs overlooking the Mississippi, was the only Confederate stronghold along the entire river that refused to fall to Union land and river forces.

By mid-May 1863, Vicksburg was surrounded by Federal gunboats in the river and Grant's army on the land. Then, on May 15, 1863, shells began to rain down upon the city.

Young Lucy McRae was one of the thousands of civilians who endured 40 days of constant bombardment, death, and starvation in that besieged city.

Diary of Death

My name is Lucy McRae. I am 13 and adore writing, which is a good thing, for there is little else to do in these endless days of sitting in terror as our town is blown apart. The exploding shells rain from the sky. Sometimes 20 in a minute. Sometimes only one or two an hour. But they always come to torment us—all day and almost all night.

Escape from Vicksburg was impossible. A vast Union army, a sea of blue, rings Vicksburg on the eastern land side (held out of town by Pemberton's soldiers in their deep trenches), just as muddy brown river water and black dots of gunboats ring us on the west. Field artillery shells with their high-pitched whine and mortar shells, a hoarse bellowing sound, now join the gunboats in pounding death and destruction onto Vicksburg. We are surrounded by a circle of fire!

When the shelling on May 29 completely destroyed our house and collapsed our small private cave, we moved into one of the large caves dug deep into the yellow clay hillside below Sky Parlor Hill. Mother wept all day and could not be consoled. Over and over she cried, "Why must they destroy everything I love? What have *I* done to them? Why can't they take their fight somewhere else and leave us in peace?"

No one had an answer to any of her questions. We sat in shock in the pitch-black cave, feeling the ground quiver with each explosion.

We listened to the whines, the screeches, the thunder, and the occasional screams from those hit—or almost hit—by the bursting shells.

The elderly Groome sisters moved into our cave on June 1. Both white haired and widowed, they sat beside each other through the long days of shelling. Whenever a shell exploded near our cave, Ethel would ask, "Sister, are you killed?"

"Guess not. I can still talk," answered Eleanor. "And you?"

"Guess not. I can still hear."

Then they would both laugh at the absurdity of it all.

After two days of their unending—and unchanging—prattle, I began to wish a shell *would* strike them. Then I cursed myself for harboring such awful thoughts.

Eleanor was killed the next day by a mortar shell while carrying a bucket of water. With vacant, lost eyes, Ethel now sits alone by the cave entrance and quietly says both sides of the conversation whenever a shell strikes nearby. I dare not get annoyed at her for it. I don't want any more blood on my hands!

Mr. Cantwell, who lived down the street from us, was shaking hands good morning with a friend when an exploding shell left him splattered with blood and holding a disembodied hand. A 13-month-old girl was killed while taking her first steps. Both parents cheered as their baby girl struggled to walk, and then screamed when a shell ended her life.

Can any terror be worse than this horrible shelling? Oh, God, how I wish it would stop, just for one day, for even one hour of peace!

Mrs. Willis was changing a leg dressing on a wounded soldier when a mortar shell crashed through the wall and killed him where he lay. Later that same day she was holding the hand of a badly wounded man when a bursting shell sent shrapnel through the wall and killed *him*. Now she trembles uncontrollably and moans so piteously, many fear she will die of pure grief.

Mrs. Reyers had, with great satisfaction, just finished tending a row of eight soldiers lying in adjacent beds when an explosion collapsed the wall, killing all eight. She ran into the street screaming and was killed by the next shell.

May Green has three small children. Her husband is away with General Johnson's army somewhere in Tennessee. She has grown exhausted, chasing after her rambunctious boys. With the constant rumble of shellings, they have become unable to sit still. Brad, her six-year-old, got away, but couldn't have been out of the long, T-shaped cave more than five minutes when four of us ran out to search. Emma Balfour found him dead and buried under a pile of smoldering rubble. Now May can't stop sobbing and trembling. Other women have had to take care of May's two remaining boys.

June 10. I am no longer sure there is an outside world. We have been completely cut off from supplies and news for almost a month. Does the world know we are still here—and suffering unimaginable tragedies every day?

Food is critically low. No one gets more than one meal a day. Gnawing hunger is a more constant and disturbing companion than is the endless shelling.

I made a trip to the nearest well to fetch our family's bucket of water for the day. (No one is allowed to wash any longer. With 31,000 soldiers and we civilians, the wells are quickly running dry.) Along the way I noticed that all the birds are gone. Not one song, not one twitter could I hear. The traitors! They have all defected to the Union side where trees and grass still grow unmolested.

I might want to join them, but we have all resolved never to surrender. I am now convinced that we will eventually all be killed by the shelling—a few at a time, day after day, until there is no one left to shoot at. With thousands of shells falling on us every day, it seems a mathematical certainty that one will eventually hit me.

June 15. There is no food. How can we survive if we can't eat? Babies chew on dirt. Mothers don't even stop them anymore. Better dirt in their bellies than nothing at all. As awful as it sounds, we have all resorted to eating mule. It's not bad, but there isn't much left. There are no vegetables. All the gardens in town have been destroyed by shelling.

We had a weed salad last night. It was spiny, bitter, and terrible tasting. I almost gagged. But at least it was *something*. The rock-hard pea bread we have been eating and sweet potato coffee are also gone. There was a fistfight over a single moldy apple yesterday. Two men went to the hospital because of the injuries they received. One of them later died—all for one moldy apple! The other supposedly shrugged and said, "One less mouth to feed." I am too tired from terrible hunger to march out to the hospital and see if it is true.

June 18. The sun is out. Maybe I'll be lucky and find a juicy rat and we will live for one more day.

FOR FURTHER READING

Here are a few good books to let you read more about the Civil War in the west and the fall of Vicksburg.

Bearss, E. *The Campaign for Vicksburg* (4 vols.). Dayton, OH: Morningside Press, 1995.

Burns, K. *The Civil War* (nine-part video series). Washington, DC: PBS Video, 1996.

Carter, S. *The Final Fortress: The Campaign for Vicksburg, 1862–1863.* New York: St. Martin's Press, 1996.

Haven, K. *Voices of the American Civil War*. Westport, CT: Libraries Unlimited, 2002.

Heathcotte, T. *Vicksburg*. London: Brassey Books, 2004.

Hoehling, A. *Vicksburg: 47 Days of Siege*. Englewood Cliffs, NJ: Prentice Hall, Inc., 1999.

See your librarian for additional titles.

Sounding Battle

The Life of a Drummer Boy at the Battle of Chicka-mauga, September 1863

This story is extracted with publisher's permission from a story of the same name in *Voices of the American Civil War* (Libraries Unlimited, 2002). See *Voices of the American Civil War* for the complete story and for additional references and follow-up activities.

ABOUT THIS STORY

Rarely do we picture 12- and 13-year-old drummer boys marching bravely into battle with Civil War lines of soldiers or think of the practiced sound of regimental drum signals.

However, both sides of the Civil War used drummer boys. Regimental drummers were supposed to be at least 16. Battalion or company drummers were often as young as 12—a few as young as 10. Some of these boys were treated as mascots, some like regular soldiers. Regimental drummer boys were paid a regular soldier's wage. Drummer boys for smaller units were paid with whatever their unit could raise.

Late in the summer of 1863, Confederate General Braxton Bragg's army of 55,000 faced Federal General William Rosecrans with his 50,000 men near a meandering creek in northwest Georgia called the Chickamauga. For brand-new Confederate drummer Ephram Dillard, this was a first peek at both Union soldiers and the sights, sound, frenzy, and terror of battle.

The generals and events depicted in this story are factual and historically accurate. The character of Ephram Dillard is based on a real southern drummer boy. Specific dialogue has been created for the story but is based on available historic records, diaries, and letters.

Sounding Battle

"We're going to fight at *night*, sir?"

"Steady, boy. Sound advance."

Efi pounded on his drum to signal each company in the regiment to advance. But Efi heard his heart pounding far louder than his drum. He felt that his feet floated above the ground, and that the deep blues, grays, and blacks of the twilight woods and fields drifted by in a dream.

Off to his right, Efi saw the first flickering flashes of Federal musket fire. Just a few pickets caught by surprise and firing before they fell back to their unit lines. To Efi, each flash looked like magical, sparkling fireflies twinkling in the night. "It's beautiful," he whispered.

"Steady, boy. Keep the beat steady."

Confederate cannon opened fire, the shells screeching overhead in great arches like comets before exploding in brilliant star bursts of light in the woods and Federal lines.

Thick lines of firefly musket shots ahead marked the Union troops through the dark. Exploding cannon shells lit up the night like a dazzling fireworks show. The noise of battle rose to a shattering, terrifying roar. Still, Efi thought it was the most beautiful sight he had ever seen—a magical fireworks light show staged just for him.

"Signal the regiment to halt and fire," commanded the Colonel. "One volley only."

Efi changed the pattern of his drumming and heard company commanders down the line verbally repeat the command.

The world seemed to explode in a deafening thunder; a thick, choking smoke; and a blinding flash as the 18th Mississippi's 800 guns lit up the night and hurled a deadly wave of lead at the waiting Federals.

A high-pitch, murderous wail erupted from the Confederate line, the famous rebel yell. Efi trembled at the monstrous shriek being made by so many desperate throats. It seemed to rattle the trees. Grass seemed to bend away in terror in the shadowed dark.

The rebel line advanced into trees. Muskets exploded everywhere around Efi. He stumbled and banged into a gnarled trunk, unable to see. Men screamed, cursed, cried, and fought all around him. The woods filled with firefly puffs as musket balls whined thick and deadly through the dark.

One bullet sizzled so close to Efi's ear, he could hear it sing. But still he pounded his drum in a trance-like fury. Somewhere nearby men fought with knives and fists. The losers screamed and died. The winners just screamed. And on they marched deeper into the Federal lines.

Around him, all was flashes of light, yelling, and confusion. Men ran past Efi, looking like gray shadows. Efi couldn't tell which side they were on. Musket balls whined through the night searching for victims. Leaves fell like rain as deadly lead clipped through the branches.

The first icy inklings of fear crept over Efi. He had no idea where he was, or where Col. Wood was, or even where the Confederate army was. All was just noise and firefly flashes, chaos, screams, and the steady, wounded sound of his drum as he pounded and marched, unsure of which direction he was walking.

Suddenly Efi's drum seemed to have picked up an echo. Efi stopped when his drum bumped smack into another drum in the dark. Efi leaned forward struggling to see who he'd hit as all around men screamed and musket balls screeched through the trees.

Efi could just make out a cocked blue cap and blue coat that now appeared pure black. Under the cap were two wide eyes filled with a mix of terror and fierce anger. Drumsticks were raised in his hands, as if he had been stopped in the middle of a drumbeat.

For a frozen moment the two drummer boys paused, drum to drum, as the nighttime bloody battle roared and raged around them. The Federal boy yelled and swung his drumstick forward, whacking Efi hard in the side of his head. Efi stumbled sideways, then screamed his miniature version of the rebel yell, and lunged forward with his own stick, catching the Federal boy in the throat.

The Union drummer boy staggered back, gagging. Efi screamed his rebel yell and crashed forward into his private enemy. The two rolled on the ground, awkwardly held apart by their drums.

A lightning-bright flash and a deafening roar exploded near Efi's head. The Federal drummer gasped and slumped quiet and still on the forest floor.

"Shortbread, that you?" Ace Lyman peered through the dark at Efi. "You all right?"

Efi stumbled to his feet, gasping for breath, legs trembling. "Ace, you *killed* him!"

"Him and about a dozen of his friends! I *love* this fighting!"

The captain emerged from the gloom, pistol and sword in his hands, face smeared with gunpowder and sweat. "Captain Stalter, sir," sang Ace Lyman. "Shortbread here bagged himself a Federal drummer boy. Beat him to death with his sticks, I reckon."

The captain nodded. "Well done, lad. Well done, indeed." He paused to assess the chaotic fighting still pounding through the woods. "It's too dark to continue. Signal regimental assembly call."

Hands trembling, Efi mechanically pounded the signal on his drum.

Company commanders slowly gathered. A few fires were lit. Efi found four bullet holes in his drum, two in his coat, and a stinging red welt on his temple from the northern drumstick. A thin trickle of blood even dribbled down his face from where a twig had gouged him.

He dabbed blood away with a sleeve, creating a red smear on his coat, and suddenly swelled with the proud feeling of being a soldier. He felt a sudden bond, a brotherhood, a fierce closeness with these scruffy men huddled around him.

Col. Wood emerged from the dark and called, "Where's the drummer boy?"

"We got no *boys* here, Colonel," answered Sgt. Mace Williams, still tending a bullet wound in his arm that had soaked his sleeve with blood. "Anyone who could survive through a night like this, why, they must be a *man*, not a boy."

Even as he swelled with a fierce pride and swaggered to his feet, Ephram wished with all his heart that he could go back to being a boy.

FOR FURTHER READING

Here are a few good books to let you read more about the role of drummer boys in the Civil War.

Arnold, J. *Chickamauga, 1863*. Westport, CT: Praeger, 2004.

Cohn, S. *Beyond Their Years*. Guilford, CT: Twodot Books, 2003.

Damon, D. *Growing Up in the Civil War*. Minneapolis, MN: Lerner Books, 2003.

Haven, K. *Voices of the American Civil War*. Westport, CT: Libraries Unlimited, 2002.

Murphy, J. *The Boy's War*. New York: Clarion, 1996.

Time-Life Books, eds. *Voices of the Civil War: Chickamauga*. Alexandria, VA: Time-Life Books, 1988.

See your librarian for additional titles.

Juneteenth
The Last Slaves to Be Notified of Their Freedom on June 19, 1865

ABOUT THIS STORY

Abraham Lincoln's Emancipation Proclamation officially freed all southern slaves on January 1, 1863. General Robert E. Lee surrendered his Army of Northern Virginia on April 9, 1865, effectively ending southern resistance to northern rule and laws. The last battle of the Civil War was fought 10 days later in western North Carolina. The Civil War was over. So, officially, was slavery.

However, few plantation owners voluntarily told their slaves—slaves that these owners thought of as mere property— that they were free. Free to leave, free to stay, free to work in the fields, free to work at a trade, or free to not work at all. Someone had to force each owner to inform his or her former slaves of their new rights and freedoms.

The army was assigned the task of notifying all former slaves of their new freedom. That word did not reach the last holdout corner of the slave plantation world in northeast Texas until June 19, 1865. On that day army units under the command of General Gordon Granger fanned out across east Texas to notify the last slaves in America that they were free. Slavery finally ended. The Turner plantation was one of the places the army reached that day.

The characters and events in this story are historically accurate. The specific dialogue is fiction but based on available historic records.

Juneteenth

A crowd of blacks had gathered below the columned front porch when Mamma Bell (a 40-year-old field worker) arrived. Bull (who'd tried to run and now dragged an iron ball welded onto one leg to keep him from running again) and Thomas (whose leg had been badly broken six years earlier) dragged in a minute later. Eight Yankee soldiers looking bone-weary and dust covered slouched on their horses.

A young lieutenant with yellow stripes down his blue pants, gleaming sword dangling at his side, read from a rolled-up piece of paper. Behind him Master Theodore Turner and his daughter, Mistress Julie, huddled together in chairs, looking confused and frightened. "… By order of General Gordon Granger and by Proclamation signed by President Lincoln on 22 September, 1862, all slaves in the state of Texas are hereby declared to be free."

The lieutenant paused for the expected cheer. All he heard was stunned silence. He raised his voice. "I said you're free. Now go on! You're free to go." He nailed the notice to a porch column with the butt of his pistol.

Eight-year-old Ellen Mae tugged at Bell's skirt. "What's dat 'free' mean, Mamma Bell?"

"It means we's free to do what we wants and go where we wants."

Ellen Mae thought for a moment. "I wants candy and a horse ride."

The adults laughed, Mamma Bell leaning far back, her whole belly shaking.

"No one gwine give you nothin'," growled Bull.

Bell hugged Ellen Mae and said, "What Bull say is true, chil'. This 'free' jus' mean won't be nobody tellin' us what we *gots* to do and where we *gots* to go no more."

Ellen Mae looked even more confused. "Then, where do we wants ta go, Mamma Bell?"

Bell shook her head, as if to clear it. "I don' rightly know. I never got to choose before."

"An' what do we want ta *do*, Mamma Bell?"

"Don't know that either, chil'." Then Bell began to laugh. "But, Lawd, I think I am surely gonna enjoy the deciding!"

Master Turner stepped forward. "None of you knows how to earn a living without me. None of you knows where you'd go or what you'd do, or how you'd earn money to eat. I'm the one who has provided all that for you. I always have, and I always will. You can stay right here and work the land with me. Go back to your homes and talk it over."

The slave's "homes" were a double row of flimsy, dirt-floor shacks with mud to cover up the gaps in the walls. Tremors of joy rumbled through the shocked cluster of 80 blacks that milled around the open space between the rows of shacks. Freedom had always been a dream, a distant beacon of light, something for the next life, or at least something you had to work, risk, and plan for. Now this dust-covered, blue-coated lieutenant had dumped it in their laps.

"I still don' believe it," muttered Bull. "You'll see. It's gwine be a trick."

"Naw, it's true," said Hector. "I heard 'em talkin' 'bout that paper at the big house las' summer. Jus' didn't believe it." Hector was a powerful mountain of a man. He worked as a gardener at the big house. Hector was the only slave on the plantation who could read.

"If'n I's free," Bull asked, "do I still gotta wear this iron ball?"

"I s'pose only if you wants to."

Bull crossed his thin arms. "Les' jus' find out how free is free." He raised his voice to be heard over the rumble of other conversations. "Joseph Henry, is your blacksmith forge still hot?"

Joseph Henry was a thick-armed, chocolate-brown man with a wide nose that seemed to spread out wider than his mouth. He seldom spoke and seldom smiled. "I s'pose."

"Then chisel this here leg iron off me. Ain't no feelin' free wid this here leg iron."

"But the sheriff hisself put that thing on!"

"He put it on a slave," corrected Bull. "If'n I ain't no slave, den this here thing can come off."

Joseph Henry rubbed his chin while he thought. "If I's free, guess I can run the forge when I wants. Let's go."

In a daze, Bell repeated, "Dat pres'dent freed us in '62…. All dis time we was free and never know'd it. Almos' three years we've been actin' like slaves when we was really free…. Three years!"

"What you gonna do?" asked Aunt Pearl, who cooked in the big house.

"I'm gwine burn down the big house an' everyone in it," Bull growled, beginning this final dragging of his hated chain toward the blacksmith's shop.

"You do dat, an' you get shot real quick," answered Bell.

"I think I'm gonna burn me this here shack," said Thomas, pointing with his thumb at the hut where he slept.

"What you gonna burn your own house fo'?" exclaimed Pearl.

"This here is a slave's house. An' if I ain't no slave no more, then I ain't gonna sleep in a slave's house."

Wringing her hands as if overcome with the enormity of the decisions now facing her, Pearl repeated, "What you *really* gonna do?"

Hector said, "I hear some is plannin' to go west. But that paper da' soldiers tacked on da' porch say if we stay, we gits 40 acres and a mule. I could do me right nice with my own 40 acres an' a mule."

"*Everybody* get that, or jus' 40 acres for all of us?" asked Thomas.

"Blue coats say the gov'ment gwine ta give 40 acres to anyone who wants it."

Thomas whistled, "To *anyone*? Lawd! I didn't knows there was that much lan' in the whole worl'."

Aunt Pearl said, "I'm goin' with those soldiers this very night. I don't know 'xactly where they's goin, but anywhere is better than this place, and anything I do *there* is better than still livin' *here*."

Bell asked, "What day is this?"

Hector answered, "Massa's wall calendar say …"

Bull interrupted, "He ain't no massa no more if'n we ain't slaves no more. He's jus' a howdy-do Mr. Turner."

Hector shrugged. "The big house wall calendar say June 19."

"June de' nineteenth," repeated Bell. "I am surely gonna remember me this date!" Her face spread into a wide grin and she swept forward to the middle of the crowd. "Well, I know what *I'm* gonna do. Right here, right now. I am gonna dance the first free dance of my life. You jus' stan' back an' watch how high a free woman can kick up her heels!"

FOR FURTHER READING

Here are a few good books to let you read more about the Juneteenth Celebration and the end of slavery in America.

Burns, K. *The Civil War* (nine-part video series). Washington, DC: PBS Video, 1996.

Ellison, R. *Juneteenth*. New York: Random House, 1999.

Gray, H. *A Time to Be Remembered: The Juneteenth Story*. Palo Alto, CA: AJH Video Productions, 1993.

Leeper, A. *Juneteenth: A Day to Celebrate Freedom from Slavery*. Berkeley Heights, NJ: Enslow, 2004.

Preszler, J. *Juneteenth*. Arlington, VA: First Fact Books, 2006.

Schroder, M. *Juneteenth (On My Own Holidays)*. Bel Air, CA: First Avenue Editions, 2006.

Taylor, C. *Juneteenth: A Celebration of Freedom*. Seattle, WA: Open Hand Publications, 2002.

See your librarian for additional titles.

Cold, Dark, and Deadly
A Cabin Boy's Efforts to Save a Ship from Sea Monsters, 1888

This story is extracted with publisher's permission from a story of the same name in *That's Weird! Awesome Science Mysteries* (Fulcrum, 2001). See *That's Weird! Awesome Science Mysteries* for the complete story and for additional references and follow-up activities.

ABOUT THIS STORY

Virtually every ancient map of the seas shows evil, monstrous sea serpents lurking near the fringes. Every seafaring culture has a trove of stories of desperate encounters with giant sea creatures—some like snakes, some like giant dragons, some like slithering tentacled squid, some like dinosaur-era oceanic reptiles. Literally thousands of sightings and attacks by giant sea serpents have been well documented through the ages.

Are there really giant creatures lurking in the sea lanes waiting to attack?

The sinking of the *Carolyn* is listed in old naval records. There was a board of inquiry called, partly for insurance purposes, partly to determine if Johnny Longden was murdered on the life raft or not. The account presented here is based on the statements by the three survivors of the wreck. I have created specific dialogue since they did not include it in the official report.

Cold, Dark, and Deadly

The *Carolyn* was a merchant ship sailing full out of Halifax, Nova Scotia, bound for Baltimore in August 1888. A trim schooner, she struggled through unusually calm seas for the north Atlantic with both masts rigged fore and aft trying to catch any puff of breeze that might wander by. She rode deep in the water, carrying 190 tons of cargo and a crew of 18.

As the sun set in a great orange ball, leaving the cloudless sky to the stars, the ship's bell clanged eight times, the tones floating across an empty ocean. Eight bells were the universal signal for a crew change.

Johnny Longden, ship's mate, stood at the helm. "New deck crew up the rigging. Tighten all ratlines." His voice always sounded thin and whiny. But rat-faced Johnny Longden was as mean as a ferret and as tough as a wolverine.

"What's the point?" grumbled Jefferson Kitlers (a short, powerful black man the crew called "Kit"). "There's no wind to catch."

Longden muttered, "I don't like a sea with no wind. Evil things happen on a flat sea at night."

The four crewmen coming off duty massaged rope coils into comfortable chairs and lounged on the deck. It was still too stuffy down below from the heat of the day.

Ned Billings slid his harmonica out of a pocket and began to play. Ned was only 25, but had been called "Old Ned" since he first joined the *Carolyn* four years ago. Jerimiah Coglin, the cook, and Billy Wolf, ship's cabin boy, hustled up onto deck, wiping their hands on aprons, to listen.

Billy's head snapped to the left. Movement caught the corner of his eye. There! A hump rising slightly out of the water 100 yards off the port bow.

There it was again. A dark-gray mound gliding through the calm waters. "Lookie there!" he cried. "Somethin's out there."

The music stopped. Most dashed to the rail and squinted into the darkness following Billy's pointing finger.

"I don't see nothing."

"It was there, I tell ya! A big hump … well, a *something*."

Most crewmen laughed and shook their heads.

Jerimiah Coglin chided, "Maybe the hump you saw, young Billy, was a bloody *wave*." The sailors burst into a new round of laughter. "A wave in the ocean would be worth pointin' out, all right!"

As he slid back down the ropes to the deck, Kit eased over to Billy and said in a low voice, "I didn't see it, Billy, but I believe it. Nights such as this, with a hot, calm sea and not a breath of air, it drives sea serpents crazy and turns them mean."

"I've seen 'em, too," said Samuel Withers, the Canadian, in a soft, solemn voice. "On the St. Lawrence. Something big and black glided up next to our ship. It was longer than I could see. Then it darted off. Our whole ship pitched and rolled in its wake."

A rumbling vibration ran through the ship, sounding like the keel scraping over an uncharted mud shoal. Every sailor froze, bracing himself against deck and rail for another shock wave.

Captain James Blanchard stormed onto the deck wearing only the red long johns he slept in and carrying his cutlass. "What in blazes did you run us into, Mr. Longden?" Captain Blanchard was a giant bear of a man who could out-wrestle any two of his crew. He growled and snarled like a bear, but every man who served under him knew him to be fair and kind, and to possess a flawless "sixth sense" about the sea.

"We're in open sea a hundred miles from shore," Mr. Longden protested. "There's nothing out here to hit."

"Well, *something* bumped against my ship," snarled the captain.

The *Carolyn* lifted slightly higher in the water and rolled ominously to starboard.

"By thunder!" Captain Blanchard roared. "No sea monster is taking my ship." He clanged the ship's bell. "All hands to deck! Break out the ship's arms. Grab pikes and axes. Man the rails."

The *Carolyn* stopped dead in the water, as if a giant hand suddenly held it back. Timbers creaked. Spars and ropes groaned. The deck shuddered.

Except for the gentle lapping of tiny waves, not a sound broke the eerie silence for several long minutes. Hearts pounded. Mouths turned desert dry. Old Ned tried to play his harmonica, but he found his mouth too dry to blow and his hands trembling too much to play a clear note.

The *Carolyn*'s bow dipped as if starting down a hill. The crew all wailed, "Whoooooooa!" and grabbed tight to whatever was near.

"I see arms, Cap'n," called young Billy Wolf, hanging over the bow rail. "They've grabbed the bow."

"Well, shoot the arms, by thunder!" roared the reply.

Young Billy was the first to lean over the rail and fire at the monster.

"Cap'n, I see a giant eye. Bigger'n my whole head!" called Henry. "It's lookin' at me."

"Well, shoot it, man!"

Henry raised his single-shot pistol. But before he could steady himself, aim, and fire, a thick tentacle whipped over the rail and wrapped around Henry's waist. Thick as a mast and long as a coiled rope, the tentacle hoisted him high in the air as if he weighed no more than a feather.

Stout Samuel Withers dove at the wiggling appendage, sinking his knife deep into its flesh. The tentacle recoiled, snapping back across the rail. Samuel was thrown overboard. Still wrapped tight, Henry disappeared with a final scream into the black sea.

Samuel didn't make it halfway up the side of the ship before two thick tentacles locked onto his legs. As if he had no more strength than a child's doll, he was sucked underwater faster than he could cry out for help.

Again all was calm and quiet on the sea. A long, terrifying minute of silence followed.

Faster than men could cry the alarm, three tentacles rose over the starboard rail. Two men fired shots into the water at the tentacle's base. One tentacle wrapped around a crewman's neck and snapped him into the water. One man hacked at a slithering tentacle with an ax until he was flung far out to sea. Jerimiah Coglin raced across the deck and finished the job, severing the tentacle with his long cleaver.

The monster withdrew. But two more in the crew were gone. Thirty feet of rubbery, severed tentacle flailed about on the deck.

Ned reached out to touch it. In a final spasm, the thing snapped around his legs, locking him tight. It took three men to pry him free of the appendage.

Five thick and deadly tentacles curled up to lock onto the ship's side and rail. The *Carolyn* rolled hard to port. Ropes, men, and supplies tumbled across the deck. Heavy cargo crates crashed across the hold, smashing into the wooden hull and springing several leaks.

Five men were flung into the sea as the grotesque monster tightened its grip on the *Carolyn*. One mast collapsed under the violent strain, crashing to the deck. Ropes and sheets fluttered down to trap the remaining crew.

Enraged, Captain Blanchard struggled to his feet and lurched across the deck toward the slimy tentacles, his cutlass in one hand, a long pike in the other. He jammed his sword clear through one tentacle to pin it to the rail. Terrified Billy Wolf hacked at the limb's slithering end near the main hatchway.

Razor-sharp pike in hand, the captain dove overboard into the heart of the frothing mass of tentacles to attack the beast. Sharks appeared and began to circle, hoping to feed on the scraps.

The rail dipped below water line. Ocean water rushed into open hatchways and sloshed into the cargo hold. Clinging to the broken mast stub, Ned could clearly see past the seething tentacles to a sharp and metal-hard beak that clicked and churned the water, eager to devour every living creature on the ship. He saw no sign of the captain, only his pike jammed into the side of the monster's gaping mouth.

The *Carolyn* was sinking. There was no longer any way to save her. Old Ned and Kit tore at the main hatch cover to loosen it from its hinges. Ned grabbed Billy Wolf by the collar and dove onto this makeshift raft as the deck sank below the rippling waves. Johnny

Longden flung himself on just before the raft drifted clear of the wreck.

The four sailors huddled together, adrift in a sea of circling sharks, as ship and monster both disappeared with a final swirling gurgle into the deep.

Three days later two men and a cabin boy were plucked from the ocean by a passing ship. First mate Johnny Longden had mysteriously disappeared in the night. The three survivors all agreed on every detail of their frightful encounter with the Kraken—except on how Mr. Longden had disappeared, which remained, forever, an unsolved mystery.

FOR FURTHER READING

Here are a few good books to let you read more about sea serpents and sea monsters in seafaring history.

Abrahamson, D. "Elusive Behemoth: Giant Squid." *Rodale's Scuba Diving*. October 1998: 106–118.

Bright, M. *There Are Giants in the Sea*. London: Robson Books, 1999.

Ellis, R. *Monsters of the Sea*. New York: Alfred Knopf, 2006.

Haven, K. *That's Weird! Awesome Science Mysteries*. Boulder, CO: Fulcrum Resources, 2001.

McKerley, J. *The Kraken*. Chicago: KidHaven Press, 2007.

Peattie, N. *Hydra and Kraken, or, the Lore and Lure of Lake-Monsters and Sea-Monsters*. Oakland, CA: Regent Press, 1998.

Pirotta, S. *Monsters of the Deep*. New York: Thomson Learning, 1996.

Sautter, A. *Sea Monsters*. Portland, OR: Blazers, 2006.

See your librarian for additional titles.

Stroke, Breathe, Kick, Glide
Gertrude Ederle's Swim across the English Channel, August 1926

This story is extracted with publisher's permission from a story of the same name in *Amazing American Women* (Libraries Unlimited, 1995). See *Amazing American Women* for the complete story and for additional references and follow-up activities.

ABOUT THIS STORY

The English Channel separating France and England has always been called treacherous. It's waters are cold and choppy. Its currents run strong and dangerous. Storms brew up fast with howling winds.

Still, long-distance swimmers have been drawn to this channel as the ultimate test of swimming endurance. No one completed the 20-plus mile swim between England and France until 1875. By 1925 only five had made the crossing, though many had tried.

Then a small American girl tried. She became the first woman to swim the English Channel in history. The characters and events in this story are historically accurate. The specific dialogue is fiction but based on available historic records.

Stroke, Breathe, Kick, Glide

August 6, 1926, dawned cool and windy on the Normandy coast of France. But at least it was clear. In the cramped hotel room she used as a training headquarters, 19-year-old Gertrude Ederle didn't feel nervous or apprehensive. She felt impatient and anxious to get in the water and get on with the swimming.

Gertrude's least favorite part of long swims in frigid water was the greasing she had to endure to keep out the cold. Her sister, Margaret, was there to help. First a one-eighth-inch-thick layer of lanolin spread evenly head to toe, then a thick layer of heavy grease. Only then could Gertrude slip into her bright red bathing dress with matching red skullcap and goggles. Then Margaret slathered the final layer of heavy grease over the top, again head to toe.

With a final stretch, Gertrude stepped into the water at 7:09 AM. Trays of photo flash powder exploded all around her. "It was almost like fireworks for a send-off," she thought.

When the chilly water reached waist deep, Gertrude dove forward and started her strong, steady crawl stroke. Timing clocks clicked on.

Stroke, breathe, kick, glide; stroke, kick, glide. Stroke, breathe, kick, glide; stroke, kick, glide.

As Gertrude reached the escort tugs, her swimming coach, William Burgess, leaned over the side and yelled, "You're doing 30 strokes a minute, Miss Ederle. Too fast. Slow down and save your strength."

Stroke, breathe, kick, glide; stroke, kick, glide. Gertrude felt incredibly powerful, invincible. Thirty strokes a minute suited her just fine. She just might speed up to 32.

On the press's tug, cameras and flash trays dangled over the side. Pencils busily scribbled.

Stroke, breathe, kick, glide; stroke, kick, glide.

Gertrude's coach, father, and sister huddled over charts and tide tables. "How far will she have to swim?" asked Mr. Ederle.

Burgess pointed to the charts. "It's 21 miles straight across. But with these currents and tides dragging her about, I figure she'll actually have to swim just over 26."

Gazing at the steady strokes of his daughter 20 feet off the port side of their tug, Mr. Ederle nervously rubbed his forehead. "Twenty-six miles.... That's a long way, even for Gertrude."

Stroke, breathe, kick, glide; stroke, kick, glide. Time and place ceased to hold any meaning for Gertrude. There was only the endless salt water, the seamless flow of her arms, the slow, steady kick of her feet, and the clockwork rolling of her head: left to breathe, down to glide and exhale. Fifteen times a minute—every other stroke—roll left to breathe, down to glide and exhale.

Three-foot windswept swells began to buffet Gertrude about noon. Often her head rolled left to breathe and found itself still well under the surface of a wave crest. Sometimes her head rolled down to glide and found itself looking down to the water surface as she popped out of a wave and over a trough.

Gertrude's progress slowed to a crawl. Most of her effort was wasted in riding up and down with the waves instead of forward to Dover. It was hard to hold her rhythm. Each stroke began to feel like an individual effort.

At 12:30 Mr. Ederle flipped on the radio to announce that Gertrude had crossed mid-channel, well ahead of the world record pace. The news flashed to radio stations around the world and to electronic billboards in Times Square. Cars honked their horns. Pedestrians stopped and cheered.

Stroke, breathe, kick, glide; stroke, kick, glide. Gertrude couldn't remember walking on dry land anymore. It felt like the whole world had always been water.

By 4:00 the sun was lost behind heavy, black clouds. The wind had risen to a steady moan, whipping the sea into an endless field of choppy whitecaps. Both tugs rolled and pitched. Any loose equipment rolled across the decks.

Stroke, breathe, kick, glide; stroke, kick, glide.

"Land ho!" cried the lookout. Half the shipboard crowd rushed to the rails to gaze west-northwest at the white cliffs of Dover. The other half yanked on pocket-watch chains to check the time.

"Gracious. It's only 5:20!" cried Mr. Ederle. "She's way ahead of the record."

"Aye, but she looks frightfully tired to me," said Burgess.

"Of course, she's tired," snapped Mr. Ederle. "She's been swimming in rough, cold water for 10 and a half hours! How much farther does she have to go?"

Burgess scowled and pointed at the chalk-white cliffs faintly rising out of the distant sea. "It's only four or so miles to those cliffs. But the currents have turned on her. Now besides that cursed wind in her face, and this dangerous chop, she's got a two-knot current driving straight into her. I don't care who she is. Fighting that combination, the cliffs might as well be 20 miles away."

As if that note were a signal to the heavens, the wind increased from a moan to a howl. The clouds seethed and rain fell, hard and cold.

Stroke, breathe, kick, glide; stroke, kick, glide. Gertrude sensed a new feeling to the water flowing around her. She raised her head, treading water for a moment. Rain. Fresh water tasted strange after so many hours of washing salt water through her mouth.

No. There was something else. As soon as she stopped kicking, she could feel herself drifting backward, farther out to sea. She was swimming into a tidal current, a strong one. All her normal swimming speed and power would be eaten up by this current. Progress toward the shore would only come from some superhuman reserve she'd have to find deep inside.

Gertrude threw herself back toward the beach, digging hard into the ebbing water with every stroke. Her hands clawed at the waves searching for handholds to pull herself toward the distant shore. Her back arched like a sprinter trying to force her way through the sea.

Wind tore the top off every wave. Flying spray mixed with rain.

Inch by inch the distant cliffs drifted by as the wind howled and rain pounded down. The sun sank toward the western horizon, lost behind thick clouds. It grew dark.

Stroke, breathe, kick; stroke, breathe, kick. There was no getting tired anymore. There was no feeling at all. There was only swimming.

A long caravan of cars, trucks, and busses streamed out of Dover, heading north to meet the swimmer. Huge bonfires were lit along the beach to light her way.

Gertrude's ears, ringing from their long pounding by the waves and salt water, heard a new sound: big and crashing, slow and rhythmic, far up ahead. Both tugs throttled back, dropping away from her.

Gertrude sluggishly wondered why. She paused and raised her head in the dark. A sea of fires, lanterns, and lights sparkled only a hundred yards ahead of her. To Gertrude they looked like a sea of stars or twinkling fairy lights.

Then it hit her. The shore! The new sound was waves breaking on a beach. She had reached England.

Weary arms mechanically plunged ahead in their unstoppable cadence. Stroke, breathe, kick. A cheering crowd waded into the sea to greet her. Gertrude's feet brushed sand. She stood in waist-deep water and waded ashore.

"Fourteen hours, 31 minutes. A new record!" yelled someone as Gertrude reached the beach.

FOR FURTHER READING

Here are a few good books to let you read more about swimming the English Channel and about Gertrude Ederle.

Adler, D. *America's Champion Swimmer*. New York: Voyager Books, 2005.

Cox, L. *Swimming to Antarctica: Tales of a Long Distance Swimmer*. Fort Washington, PA: Harvest Books, 2005.

Dean, P. *Open Water Swimming*. Champaign, IL: Human Kinetics Publishers, 1998.

Gonsalvas, K. *First to the Wall: 100 Years of Olympic Swimming*. Baltimore, MD: Freestyle Publications, 1999.

New York Times. Saturday, August 7, 1926, pages A1 and A3. Numerous articles on Gertrude Ederle's swim.

See your librarian for additional titles.

The Storm Breaks

Three Japanese American Boys' Experience of the Pearl Harbor Attack, December 7, 1941

ABOUT THIS STORY

In 1941, 130,000 Japanese Americans lived in Hawaii. They were all loyal and hard-working. The surprise Japanese attack on Pearl Harbor on December 7, 1941, was doubly catastrophic for them. Their city and country had been attacked. Yet, because they were Japanese, they became instantly the enemy. On that Sunday morning they felt that they had lost everything.

The characters and dialog in this story are fictional. However, their actions and reactions are based on interviews with actual survivors of that terrible day. Every statement relating to the attack on Pearl Harbor by Japanese air forces is historically accurate.

The Storm Breaks

Lazy puff-ball clouds glowed pale orange and yellow this quiet Sunday morning of December 7, 1941. The sun peaked past Diamond Head but had not yet chased away the soothing cool of dawn.

Eleven-year-old Ishi Ichiro slowly cranked in his fishing line. "Nothing's biting today. Maybe out deeper in the channel."

There were a few scattered shacks on this strip of sand and red Hawaiian clay between Ewa Beach and the reeds, marshes, and mud of an Ewa-side finger of the West Lock, a part of the back bay of Pearl Harbor that the Navy wasn't using. A dozen other cars were haphazardly parked on the packed sand, jammed against thick bushes and waving shore grasses.

Ishi's 18-year-old brother, Matsu, grunted—the one way in which he tried to mimic their father. "Ey! We probably no catch nothin'!" He proudly scratched the scraggly goatee he was trying to grow. "Fish all *pau* [gone] in da harbor, anyway. Da water be too stink."

A massive Hawaiian named Kimo plodded over. Kimo looked like a sumo wrestler with a bright-white smile that was almost wider than his round face. Kimo had been the Ichiros' neighbor when they lived in Pearl City.

Kimo raised the thumb and little finger of one hand. It was a general-purpose Hawaiian greeting. "No one catchin' nothin' today. What you think, Ishi? Fish really *pau?*"

All the local fishermen on the *Ewa* (western) side of Pearl Harbor agreed that Ishi Ichiro had a nose for finding fish.

Ishi cocked his head, thinking as he tugged on his line. Finally he smiled and motioned with his chin toward the deepest part of the West Loch. "They're here. But out deep, I think. In the channel."

Matsu laughed and dropped into a boxer's stance, pretending to jab and hook at Ishi. "Watchoo think you? Last Sunday you been say fish always in close, nibble yum-yum by the reeds. No fishes there today, so you make up one new story *wiki wiki!*"

Twenty-year-old Cousin Hiram Nikaido always rounded out the Sunday morning fishing party. He laughed, "Careful, Matsu. Ishi knows fish better than anyone."

A faint *boom … boom … boom* in the distance tugged at their attention.

Hiram scowled and glanced at his watch. 7:55 AM. "Early army maneuvers today—and on a Sunday."

Thump … thump … throomp…. The distant pounding seemed to grow louder and more insistent. Hiram squinted into the rising sun and pointed toward a thin black column of smoke rising in the east. "Maybe it's an industrial fire over in Iwiali."

Iwiali was an area of factories and oil storage tanks between the airport and downtown.

Thump … thump … THUMP! The booms wouldn't stop. More columns of smoke began to rise like thick, black tree trunks into the morning sky.

Hiram said, "Those look like *real* explosions!" He shaded his eyes and added, "I think that smoke is coming from Hickam."

Hickam Army Airfield was the biggest airfield in the islands and shared runways with the commercial airport.

Ishi noticed that Hiram's voice was beginning to rise, tense and anxious.

Ishi pointed high into the sky over the distant east side of Pearl Harbor. Swarms of black dots, looking like gnats, circled between popcorn-sized white puffs of exploding smoke—airplanes, circling like vultures over Honolulu.

"That looks like anti-aircraft fire," reported Hiram. "*What* is going on?"

Then the first explosion in the harbor itself, by Ford's Island, blasted across the back bay. Its concussion hammered against Ishi's chest. Its roar thundered in his ears. Ominous black smoke billowed into the sky. Dogs back in Pearl City howled in response. A pack of birds noisily flapped out of the trees.

The concussion of another explosion slammed across the fishermen with a nightmare of boiling red flames and angry smoke rising as if from a volcano.

No one spoke. The back-bay fishermen stood like frozen, gaping-mouthed statues and stared at the horror churning the main stretches of Pearl Harbor into boiling chaos. Their poles were held in unmoving hands, frozen mock salutes.

Then one of the planes roared low up their finger of the West Loch, escaping from the Navy's machine gun fire. That plane thundered over the cluster of startled fishermen less than 30 feet above the water, its engine whining so hard Ishi was sure it would tear itself apart.

That plane was painted deep amber (a greenish-golden brown), not silver like American planes. Everyone clearly saw the red circle on each wing—not white stars like on American planes. It thundered by so low that they could see white smoke trail from the plane's red-hot machine gun barrels. They could see the pilot's leather helmet, over-sized goggles, and white cloth tied around his head.

Amber paint. Red circle. "That looked like a Japanese plane," whispered Hiram, more confused than startled.

Another explosion rocked the harbor. Flames and rolling smoke gushed from another in the long line of battleships.

The fishermen could feel the concussion of each explosion pound through the still morning air. They could feel the jarring vibrations race through the mud like an earthquake and see the towering billows of smoke. They felt a growing communal fear gnaw at their stomachs. Waves of searing heat rolled across the water as if a giant blast furnace door had been opened.

Pearl Harbor and Hickam Airfield were being attacked. Anti-aircraft fire filled the sky and matched the deafening roar of the planes. The massive ships that were the pride of the American Navy were exploding in flame.

And Japanese planes were doing it!

The endless explosions blended together into a hideous dragon's roar that shook the world and brought every living thing quaking to its knees.

A Japanese plane flew toward them, black smoke streaming along its body from the front-mounted engine. Thick oil streaks smeared across the pilot's canopy. The engine sputtered as if struggling to turn over. Flames blazed past the engine cowling. Lower and lower the plane flew, its whining screech rising steadily as it sped on.

Ishi ducked as the plane thundered by so low he was sure he could have jumped and touched it. A quarter-mile inland, the plane crashed in a fireball that spewed across the coast road like a volcanic eruption and sprayed deadly metal fragments and fiery destruction into half a dozen houses at the edge of Pearl City.

Ishi staggered back to his feet, head ringing painfully from the terrible noise. Anti-aircraft fire exploded like 4th of July fireworks across the sky, like fiery rain that trickled down onto the city.

Planes crisscrossed and dove like swarms of hornets. Explosions ripped apart the morning.

Frightened fishermen clustered, searching for the safety of numbers. But without saying a word, the Chinese, Filipino, Hawaiian, and Portuguese fishermen inched away from the three Japanese, glaring at them menacingly, scornfully.

"Let's get the planes!" Ishi yelled and snatched a rock out of the mud to hurl at the next plane that raced past.

As the next plane sped toward them, the last of its machine gun bullets still burning red streaks through the air, Ishi yelled, "Get him!" and flung his rock, missing the plane's wing by over 50 feet.

His voice tense and tight, Hiram said, "Ishi, get back to the car."

"But we gotta stop the planes!" Ishi answered.

Matsu grabbed his brother's arm and hissed, "You one dummy. All *kine* danger. Run now!"

Holding his next rock, Ishi asked, "You mean from the planes?"

Hiram grabbed Ishi's other arm, spinning him around, and squeezed tight. "*Japanese* are attacking."

"So?"

Hiram hissed, "So, *think*, Ishi."

His mother often said that Ishi's brain trailed two blocks behind his mouth. But who had time to think when the world around you exploded in war? "So, that makes the Japanese the enemy and we should fight ... right?"

"Ishi, we're Japanese. *You're* Japanese."

A swirling confusion of contradictory images and ideas raced through Ishi's mind. The roar of battle made it hard to focus. "So ... ?"

The hateful glares of the other fishermen provided Ishi's answer. Matsu dragged Ishi back across mud and sand toward the short, twisting trail through waving shore grass and flowering bushes to the level spot where Matsu had parked the Ichiro family car.

The planes were flying thicker over the bay now, as if they had all gathered for the kill. The whole world seemed to explode into fire and death. A giant explosion sent the three young Japanese stumbling to their knees as its searing heat and thunder-clap concussion slammed across the bay.

Ishi turned to watch another wounded plane break through the swirling curtains of smoke and screech overhead in its own shroud of smoke and flame. Screaming its death wail, the plane crashed just above the houses along Aeia Heights. Trees and grass burst into flame.

Ishi, the last to reach the parking area, half-ran, half-stumbled toward the car with his head twisted hard over his left shoulder, staring at the boiling fire balls and smoke clouds rising over Ford's Island. Trent Sullivan crouched by the side of a sleek convertible car in the packed-sand parking area, peeking over its trunk. He sprang to his feet when he saw Ishi, his face tight with fear and hate. Trent yelled, "My brother's on one of those ships. If he's hurt, I'll *get* you. I'll get all of you lousy *Japs* for this!"

Hiram roughly shoved Ishi into the back seat and stood by the car door, trying to pretend he was a commanding officer. "We're all Americans here."

"Not you traitor Japs," screamed Trent. "Buddhaheads deserve to die!"

Matsu sprang from the driver's seat, stepping in front of Hiram. "Wot? *Haole* wants one *kine* fight? I bust you up *wiki wiki*!" Matsu stood six inches shorter and 60 pounds lighter than Trent. Still, there wasn't a trace of doubt or fear on his face.

Even friendly Kimo, who had fished with the Ichiros each week for years, glared suspiciously, jabbing a massive finger at the three Japanese. "You know 'bout this? You Japs give them some *kine* help?"

Ishi was frozen by a surging mix of fear, anger, and confusion. The *Japanese* were attacking, and suddenly everyone looked at *him* with venom and revulsion.

"I threw a rock!" he yelled back.

FOR FURTHER READING

Here are a few good books to let you read more about the Japanese attack on Pearl Harbor.

Hoyt, E. *Pearl Harbor Attack*. New York: Sterling Publishing, 2008.

McGowan, T. *The Attack on Pearl Harbor*. New York: Scholastic Library Publishing, 2007.

Santella, A. *Pearl Harbor*. Mankato, MN: Coughlan Publishing, 2004.

Sutcliffe, J. *Attack on Pearl Harbor*. Mankato, MN: Coughlan Publishing, 2006.

Tanaka, S. *Attack on Pearl Harbor*. New York: Hyperion Books for Children, 2001.

Taylor, T. *Air Raid—Pearl Harbor: The Story of December 7, 1941*. San Diego, CA: Harcourt Children's Books.

See your librarian for additional titles.

Stories from Modern Life

The Last One Fooled
April Fools' Celebration of Foolery and Pranks

This story is extracted with publisher's permission from a story
of the same name in *New Years to Kwanzaa* (Fulcrum, 1999).
See *New Years to Kwanzaa* for the complete story and for
additional references and follow-up activities.

ABOUT THIS STORY

April Fools' Day, the first day of April, is celebrated worldwide. There are no parades, no festivals, no speeches, no
organized ceremonies. Still, April 1 is looked forward to,
planned for, and enjoyed everywhere. April Fools' Day is
the only worldwide celebration that does not include any
formal ceremony, festival, or acknowledgment by religious,
governmental, or community organizations. It is a day for
foolery, for personal spontaneity, for pranks, for jokes.
Nowhere is April Fools' more enthusiastically celebrated
than in Western Europe and North America. This story
unfolded in Quebec, Canada, in 1986. But it could have
happened (and might well have) in any of 15 other countries.

The events included in this story are accurate and typical
of the mentioned events. The characters are fictional, but
are based on actual events by real people.

The Last One Fooled

Nine-year-old Eugenia Cuvier called up the curved stairway of the family's two-story row house in an older neighborhood on the west side of Montreal to her 10-year-old brother, "Arna! Breakfast!" Then she giggled and rubbed her hands together.

Eugenia slid into her seat next to the children's grandmother. "Sugar for your oatmeal?" asked Gram Methena.

"No thanks," blurted Eugenia.

"I'll have some," said Arna, settling into his seat.

Eugenia watched out of the corner of one eye as Arna scooped two heaping spoonfuls of sugar onto his cereal. He shoveled a large bite into his mouth, chewed twice, and wrinkled his face in disgust. "Bleah! This tastes terrible!"

"Want more sugar?" laughed Eugenia.

Arna's eyes widened in understanding. "It's salt! You put salt in the sugar bowl."

"April Fools!" she laughed.

"I'll get you …!" Arna reached across the table but was stopped by Gram Methena.

"Not during my breakfast, you won't." She turned to Eugenia. "Don't gloat, young lady. The day is still young, and they say that the last one fooled is the biggest fool of all."

As Arna and Eugenia stacked their dishes in the sink, Gram Methena pointed toward a corner counter. "I made some chocolate-covered fudge balls. If you call an April Fools' truce and behave today, you may both have some later."

As they headed for the door and school, Arna turned for the front closet. "I'll get your jacket, Eugenia."

Seconds later both children leapt down the front stairs, zipping jackets against the swirling wind and cold, book bags dangling from one shoulder.

Paul Moreau, a classmate of Arna's, joined them on their walk. "Hi, Arna, Eugenia." Then, *whack!* He kicked Eugenia hard in the rear.

"Ow! What was that for?!"

Paul shrugged, "Just doing what the sign says."

"What sign?" demanded Eugenia. But she didn't need the answer. She knew. Arna had already doubled over laughing. "April Fools!" he called. Then he sprinted off down the street.

Eugenia stripped off her jacket to see a large "Kick me" sign taped onto the back. "I'll get you!" she called after her brother.

At morning recess Eugenia pocketed a bottle of glue and raced to the school's cement play yard. When Arna's class was released, he sprang out the door, down the steps, and stopped dead in his tracks. "A quarter!" he cried.

He dropped to his knees and reached to scoop up the shiny coin. Then he stopped. He didn't have the quarter. He reached out a second time. Again his hand came up empty.

Other kids laughed, "Arna's too weak to lift a quarter!"

"April Fools!" cried Eugenia, leaping from behind the stairs holding her pot of glue.

"I'll get you!" screamed Arna. The other kids laughed.

Ten minutes later, Arna swaggered to where Eugenia played with three friends. There were still five minutes left in the morning recess.

"Your teacher wants to see you *now*," Arna sneered.

"Me?" gulped Eugenia. "Why?"

"Somehow he found out about your April Fools' prank."

"You told!" hissed Eugenia. "I'll get you!"

Arna grinned. "But first you have to see Mr. St. Clair."

Alone and trembling, Eugenia reentered her classroom and marched across the polished wood floor.

Mr. St. Clair's bushy eyebrows wrinkled into a frown. "What do you want?"

"You wanted to see me," answered Eugenia, her voice barely a whisper.

"About what?" demanded her teacher.

"About my April Foo ..." Then her mouth slammed shut. Her eyes widened. "Arna!" she hissed.

"Your *what?*" continued Mr. St. Clair.

"Ahhhh ... nothing, sir." Eugenia smiled, backing toward the door.

"It must be about something, young lady. Sit in your desk until either you remember or recess is over."

Blushing bright red, Eugenia sunk into her desk. Her mouth silently formed the words, "I'll get you, Arna."

At 5:30 that afternoon Gram Methena sternly summoned both children into the kitchen. A scowl etched her face. "My chocolate-covered fudge balls are gone. Which of you took them?"

"Not me," answered Arna. "Honest."

"I'd never take something of yours, Gram," stammered Eugenia.

Foot angrily tapping the linoleum floor, Gram Methena crossed her arms. "Someone here is concealing the truth. Besides me, you are the only two who have been in this house this afternoon. Now who took them?!"

Both children stared in numb shock and slowly shook their heads.

"Since no one will confess to being the thief, both of you up to your rooms and get to your homework. I will get to the bottom of this later."

Twenty minutes later, just before their parents were due home, the children were summoned downstairs. Gram Methena sat in a high-backed chair. Burly police sergeant Yves Tyers stood in his uniform in the middle of the room, hands resting on his gun belt.

The sergeant stared, grim-faced.

"Who took the fudge balls?" demanded Gram.

Arna shifted uneasily. "You called in a cop?"

Eugenia stared in silent terror at the policeman and shook her head.

"Last chance," Gram warned. "Who took them?"

Both children stared in wide-eyed terror and pleaded, "Honest. I didn't."

With a wave of her hand, Gram turned her back on her grandchildren. "Take them away, officer."

Tears streaming down her face, Eugenia stammered, "But Gram ..."

"Not a word," growled Sgt. Tyers and gestured toward the door with his head.

But Gram Methena reached under her chair and pulled out a ribboned box. She giggled, "I just remembered, *I* took them. They're right here!"

She opened the box to reveal the plate of chocolate-covered fudge balls. "April Fools!" she and Sgt. Tyers laughed, as the children's mouths dropped open.

"Now you know what a *real* April Fool feels like." And Gram extended the box. "Have one."

Arna reached in, lifted the largest fudge ball, and stuffed it into his mouth. His face wrinkled up in disgust. Around the white wad in his mouth, he cried, "Ids nod fudge. Ids cotton!"

"April Fools again!" sang Gram Methena. "And remember. The last one fooled is the biggest fool of all!"

As she tucked her grandchildren into bed that night, each one whispered, "Next year, Gram, we'll get *you*!"

FOR FURTHER READING

Here are a few good books to let you read more about April Fools' Day.

Baker, J. *April Fools' Day Magic*. Minneapolis, MN: Lerner Group, 1994.
Kelley, E. *April Fools' Day*. Minneapolis, MN: Carolrhoda Books, 1998.
Kroll, S. *It's April Fools' Day!* New York: Scholastic Trade, 1991.
Modell, F. *Look Out: It's April Fools' Day*. New York: William Morrow, 1995.
Schiller, M. *April Fools' Day*. Chicago: Children's Press, 2003.

See your librarian for additional titles.

Big Bad Wolf
A Student's Six-Month Solo Study of Arctic Wolves

This story is extracted with publisher's permission from a story of the same name in *Women at the Edge of Discovery* (Libraries Unlimited, 2003). See *Women at the Edge of Discovery* for the complete story and for additional references and follow-up activities.

ABOUT THIS STORY

In stories, wolves always represent the darkest and most evil corners of humanity—things like werewolves and the Wolfman. Folktale characters—Little Red Riding Hood, the Three Little Pigs, and Peter—all meet the embodiment of their greatest fears in a wolf. Wolves even look scary—gray creatures of the twilight with yellow slant eyes and an eerie, bone-chilling howl that sounds strangely human.

Twenty-four-year-old graduate student Rose Kellman was the only human for 80 miles in any direction across the Arctic tundra. Her 1978 six-month solo survey of the life and habits of an Arctic wolf pack was going fine until the wolf pack she was studying turned on her one night. The events included in this story are taken from her report, her articles, and her journal.

Big Bad Wolf

On May 3 Rose located the wolf pack. They had dug a den less than half a mile from her shed. Rose knew the family would stay in this territory all summer, helping the pups (born blind, deaf, and toothless) to grow into strapping 80-pound teenagers ready to survive their first Arctic winter.

Rose had shuddered when she first spotted two of the wolves loping along a ridgeline at sunset. She forced herself not to recoil in fear and run, but to follow the wolves, cautiously, ever watching for another wolf to emerge from the growing shadows behind her. At dusk she lost their trail. The next morning she was able to pick it up and follow it to the den.

Rose watched the den, the cubs, and the adult wolves through binoculars from a rock outcropping 100 yards away. In mid-afternoon, Rose bolted upright and spun around. The soft sound of breathing and padding feet through the squishy peat penetrated her fascination with the cubs. Two wolves jogged past her—less than 30 yards away—on their way to the den. Neither seemed to pay her any attention, as if in one glance they had already determined that Rose could not pose a threat. Still Rose's heart hammered in her chest and she gasped for breath. Her hands and legs trembled as she slid out of the rocks and jogged back toward her shed.

By late May, Rose began to wander at night—the wolves' primary hunting time—hoping to catch a glimpse of the wolves in action. What she saw shocked her. She carried a rifle, binoculars, and a notebook. Even from 100 yards away, Rose could hear the crunch and snap as wolves ground up and ate even the bones of their prey.

June was Rose's least favorite month in the tundra. Mosquitoes hatched, by the thousands, by the millions. Buzzing mosquitoes penetrated every fiber, every nook, every inch of ground. Rose was chased by clouds of them. There was no way to escape—either day or night—from the whining hordes of hungry bloodsuckers.

Great flocks of birds arrived to feast on the mosquitoes. Hundreds of species covered the sky in noisy rainbow profusion. The endless din of chirping and squawking reminded Rose of the constant honking clatter of big-city traffic. Sleep became a rare luxury in June.

Late on the afternoon of June 17, Rose watched from the rocks as the wolf pack gathered: two young males, two young females, and the dominant pair. Everyone wagged their tails, heads submissively low for the powerful silver-gray male who led the pack. With neck hair bristling and teeth bared, he issued warning barks and growls at each pack member to remind them of his dominance.

Then one of the wolves started the howl. All adult wolves howled in chorus, heads thrown back and mouths wide open, each adopting a different key. The seventh adult—the evening's babysitter—watched, but did not join the howl. If two wolves slid onto the same note, one quickly changed so that the different tones wove together into an eerie, human-like chorus that drifted in shimmering waves across the quiet, frozen landscape. From the far distance, a second pack of wolves answered with their own howl.

With the midnight sun hovering half below the horizon, Rose watched her wolf family surround an old and obviously sick ox. One wolf leapt at the haunches of this exhausted ox, whose wheezing breath and white, terror-filled eyes said he was too tired to resist. The wolf nipped at the hamstring muscle and bounded back to avoid the ox's hooves that instinctively lashed out with the power to splinter rock.

A second wolf sprang at the ox's muzzle, locking onto its snout as a diversion for the real attack. Two wolves raced in on the same side and crashed into the ox's rump.

It stumbled and bucked sideways, struggling to keep its balance. A fourth wolf darted in to bite and tear an Achilles' tendon in the ox's lower leg. The last wolf jumped at the ox's face, slashing at its eyes to keep it from properly reacting to the real attack behind.

Hurt, confused, and disoriented, the ox slipped on its injured back leg and sprawled to the ground. All five wolves dove to attack the now defenseless prey.

Wolves have neither the size nor power to kill quickly as a lion does. The wolves' fangs and canine teeth slashed at the ox's throat and tore at its great leg muscles. Death would come slowly as the ox's blood stained the tundra grass.

Rose watched in morbid fascination—until she heard a soft growl behind her. Rose turned to face the great silver-back male, his muzzle bright red from his attack on the ox, front legs spread, teeth bared, hair bristling. Two other wolves circled to the sides, making it impossible for her to keep them all in her field of vision.

Frantically, she glanced left and right. In the open rolling tundra there was no place to hide, nowhere to run to. Until that moment, it had never occurred to her that the wolves might attack and eat her.

Her rifle was slung on her shoulder, safety on. Even if she did swing it down to fire, she'd only stop one wolf. Yet, even in that moment of danger, Rose realized she didn't want to hurt any of these magnificent creatures she had grown to know as family.

In her hands, Rose held only a pencil with which to mount her defense. Slowly she backed away from the alpha male and away from their oxen kill. It occurred to her that she should act submissive. She began to whine and forced her eyes to gaze down at the ground in front of the snarling wolf. Step by step she inched back, bleating, whining, waiting every second to feel the same terrible attack that she had watched befall the ox.

Step by slow step, she backed away, whined, pawed at the ground with her foot, and stared at her shoes. Still growling, the wolves padded forward, keeping pace with her.

But attack never came. Once the wolves had forced her back a good 80 yards from their kill, they turned with a final howl and trotted back to enjoy their meal. They had merely wanted to make sure she didn't try to share in their conquest.

Rose trembled through the night huddled on her bed, sweating, shaking, and shivering, as she listened to the familiar drone of mosquitoes, the call of birds, and the distant howl of wolves.

FOR FURTHER READING

Here are a few good books to let you read more about arctic wolves.

Berger, M. *Howl! A Book about Wolves.* New York: Cartwheel, 2002.

Brandenburg, J. *To the Top of the World: Adventures with Arctic Wolves.* New York: Walker and Company, 1999.

Clarkson, E. *Wolf Country.* New York: E. P. Dutton & Co., 1994.

Harrington, F. *The Arctic Wolf.* New York: The Rosen Publishing Group, 2002.

Harrington, F., and P. Paquet, eds. *Wolves of the World.* Park Ridge, NJ: Noyes Publications, 1992.

Klinghammer, E., ed. *The Behavior and Ecology of Wolves.* New York: Garland STMP Press, 1993.

Lawrence, R. D. *Wolves.* San Francisco: Sierra Club Books, 1998.

Patent, D. *Gray Wolf, Red Wolf.* New York: Clarion Books, 1993.

Zimen, E., and L. Boitani. *The Wolf: A Species in Danger.* New York: Delacourt, 1996.

See your librarian for additional titles.

What a "Croc"!

Tagging Deadly Caiman in the Amazon Jungle

This story is extracted with publisher's permission from a
story of the same name in *Women at the Edge of Discovery*
(Libraries Unlimited, 2003). See *Women at the Edge of
Discovery* for the complete story and for additional
references and follow-up activities.

ABOUT THIS STORY

Caiman were slaughtered by the millions in the 20th cen-
tury when alligator shoes, boots, and bags were in fashion.
Their skins were stripped and the carcasses were left to rot
in the jungle. By 1970, caiman were extinct in 99 percent
of their historical range. Then Brazil passed laws to protect
the remaining giant predators.

Now these South American crocodiles are making a dra-
matic comeback. But science knows almost nothing about
the life cycle and habits of these mighty creatures.

Each night, researcher Karen Tejunga drifted among the
reeds of a shallow lake in her small, flat-bottom skiff, hoping
to bump into an 18-foot-long South American crocodile
(called a caiman). It's what she did for work—and for fun.

The events and actions included in this story are based on Karen's reports and on a phone interview with her.

What a "Croc"!

It's 10:30 at night on April 17, 1997, in the remote Amazon rain forest of Brazil. Twenty-nine-year-old Karen Tejunga rides in the front of a small skiff winding its way through narrow channels toward Lake Mamiraua. Her assistant sits in the back and controls the outboard motor.

Over 200 miles from the nearest road, this part of Amazonia is one of the wettest and wildest places on Earth—a land of myth and story passed through countless generations. Here, the story of the caiman (the largest and most vicious predator in the Amazon and largest crocodile in the Western Hemisphere) is frightfully short. "Caiman kill. They are the devil."

The nighttime symphony of sounds almost overpowers the whine of the tiny outboard motor—cicada, crickets, howler monkeys, birds, the howls of predators, the screams of victims, and the excited chatter of those that escape.

Karen switches on the skiff's main headlamp. Light stabs across the lake. At first it finds only water and tufts of reeds. Then the light falls on glowing dots of unearthly yellow-green. The dots always come in pairs. Karen slowly swings the light. Five, six, a dozen, then several dozen pairs of glowing dots stare back—the distant eyes of giant caiman waiting for their next meal.

Over her shoulder Karen calls, "They're thick tonight. We should be able to tag a couple."

Karen's hair is pulled back in a ponytail under the miner's helmet she wears because of its strong headlamp. She wears catcher's

shin guards, heavy gloves, and a thickly padded leather jacket—
even in this oppressive heat. She now stands barefoot in the
skiff's bow, panning the light, deciding which caiman she'll go
after.

Black and almost invisible at night, caiman can reach 22 feet long
and have four-foot hydraulic jaws that can tear a buffalo in two—or
that could crush Karen's skiff like a soda can. Caiman can live for
100 years and eat any- and everything they meet.

In the skiff Karen carries a minicassette recorder for notes, extra
batteries for the lights, two gas cans, a wire noose on an eight-foot
bamboo pole to snare caiman, lots of rope, and a bucket of tags and
radio collars. By capturing, measuring, and tagging caiman, Karen
and a few others like her hope to develop an accurate population
profile. By attaching radio collars to caiman, Karen hopes to learn
these animals' migration patterns.

But to do anything, she first has to catch them—at night.

They steer the skiff nearer to the shore. Karen clears her throat.
She breathes deeply and imitates the deep, throaty call of a caiman
bull. *Bwaaa, bwaaa, bwaaa!*

They hear a replying challenge from the dark. First one, then a
second and a third. Then a soft plop as something large slips into
the water. The glowing eyes of a young male are caught in the glare
of Karen's light.

"*That* one!" Karen calls and points with her light.

Her assistant increases the gas. The outboard whines louder. A
small wake spreads out behind the skiff. Karen flexes her knees to
keep her balance as she shines the light on the glowing yellow-green
eyes that are her target.

The skiff leaps forward as the motor whines. Karen grabs her wire noose and curls her toes tight around the edge of the wooded front seat as she braces for the attack.

The motor putters back to idle as the skiff glides along side of a 10-foot youth. Its eyes seem to glow from deep within. It appears to be sizing up Karen and the skiff for a quick meal.

Karen lowers the noose so that the bottom end of the wire loop skims along the water surface just in front of the caiman's deadly jaws. Her assistant leans over the back with a rope loop ready to snare the caiman's tail. The skiff's rail dips dangerously near to water level.

Karen lowers the noose, pulls back, and then yanks up as hard as she can in a quick and well-rehearsed motion. Her assistant loops the tail, hoists it out of the water, and throws a quick knot through an oarlock to secure it.

The caiman thrashes like a bucking Brahma bull. Water sprays as if from a fire hose. The deadly jaws, held shut by the wire noose, gnash and grind. Claws scrape at the skiff's metal side. The great body smacks against the water after it arches above the surface. The skiff rocks violently. Water sloshes over the side and flows along the flat bottom plating.

Karen speaks quickly into her recorder. "Male. Approximately 11 feet. No more than eight years. Standard mottled black pattern. No unique markings." Louder, she calls, "Help me with a collar and tag."

Her assistant kneels and reaches over the side to yank up one front leg. Karen uses a rivet gun to attach a metal tag to a loose fold of skin just above the foot. The skiff pitches and rocks as if it were caught in a violent, stormy sea. The assistant reaches into a bucket and hands Karen a radio transmitter collar that looks like an oversized dog collar. Karen loops it around the caiman's neck while her assistant bear-hugs her around the waist to keep her from pitching overboard.

"Prepare to release," Karen calls. Her assistant releases his knot in the tail rope. Karen picks up the bamboo noose pole. "Ready. One ... two ... three!" Both ends of the caiman are released. It snaps once and sinks out of sight below the surface.

Both humans sink onto the skiff's wooden bench seats to pant and thrill at their survival. Karen bails with a plastic bucket.

Gas is running low. It is after midnight. Karen signals to turn back. The outboard putters to life and they begin the hour trip back downriver to the town of Tefe, where Karen has set up her study camp.

She'll be back out tomorrow night to hunt and tag again. Maybe next time she'll catch a really *big* one. Maybe ...

FOR FURTHER READING

Here are a few good books to let you read more about caiman and the Amazon ecosystem.

Castern, James. *Layers of Life*. New York: Benchmark Press, 2001.
———. *Rainforest Researchers*. New York: Benchmark Press, 2000.
———. *River Life*. New York: Benchmark Press, 2000.
———. *Surviving in the Rain Forest*. New York: Benchmark Press, 2000.
Dollar, Sam. *Caimans*. New York: Steadwell Books, 2001.
Dorst, Jean. *The Amazon*. New York: Steck-Vaughn Library. 1998.
Lewington, Anne. *Rainforest*. New York: Raintree, Steck-Vaughn, 1999.

See your librarian for additional titles.

The Heart of the Drum
A Boy's Struggle to Find Meaning in the Tribal Celebration

ABOUT THIS STORY

The Crow Fair each August in Montana is the biggest Native American gathering in North America. The fair grew from the traditional Sun Dance Ceremony, or Sun Festival, held by virtually every Plains tribe in mid- to late summer.

Over the years that fair assumed many of the cultural needs of the Crow Nation and now draws dancers, rodeo riders, and watchers from the Incas of South America to Eskimos and Athabaskan from Alaska. As many as 10,000 attend this 20th-century ethnic spectacle, designed for both Native American and tourist alike.

The 1992 Crow Fair sprawled into a vast encampment, hugging the banks of the winding Little Big Horn River in the southeast corner of Montana. The bustling scene of the fair was a world of contrasts. Traditional angled pole and canvas or buffalo hide tepees with modern suitcases stacked outside; leather thongs and feather bustles strewn across modern, plastic lounge chairs; bare-back horse riders carrying lance and bow escorting modern RVs; blue jeans next to traditional Crow leggings.

The events included in this story are accurate and typical of the mentioned events. The characters are fictional, but are based on actual events by real people.

The Heart of the Drum

Eleven-year-old Randy Yellow Bear glumly climbed a small knoll to escape the happiness of a new Crow Fair. He felt no joy, no anticipation. He felt at loose ends, left out of the excitement. Karla, his 12-year-old sister, had the dance competition. His father would participate in important council meetings. What could *he* do that was worthwhile during this year's fair?

In the distance he heard the throbbing of several of the great drums. Often four feet across, these drums were big enough for half a dozen men to play at the same time. Singers would form a circle behind the drummers, chanting a song to the moon and stars.

But it was the pounding rhythm of 10 mallets beating on the drumheads that echoed in Randy's heart.

And then it struck him. Randy would learn to make his own drum. There was a famous drum maker at the fair, Harry Two Knives. Randy would get Mr. Two Knives to teach him to make drums that beat in the heart of every listener.

All but one drum had quieted when Randy reached the tented dance pavilion late that evening. Four drummers beat soft and slow. Their music drifted out like a lullaby to surrounding tepees.

In one corner an old man with shining silver hair sat alone, rubbing oil into a curved strip of cedar wood. His pants and vest were of well-worn deer hide with intricate designs in bright beadwork.

Randy paused, suddenly afraid to approach a revered elder of the Crow people. "Mr. Two Knives?"

"Do you play drums?" asked the old man without looking up from his work.

Randy shook his head, lowering his face in shame. "I never had a drum to play."

The old man nodded and worked oil into the wood with his fingers.

"But I *want* to," added Randy. "*If* someone will teach me how to make a drum that sings to every living heart."

Again the old man nodded. "That would be a good drum."

"Will *you* teach me?" asked Randy.

Harry Two Knives looked up, silver hair framing a worn and leathery face, piercing blue eyes searching Randy's smooth, round face. "And what would be the first song you'd play on such a drum?"

"A song of praise for my teacher!" answered Randy.

The old blue eyes clouded over. "Too bad I have forgotten how drums are made." And Harry Two Knives returned to his work.

Nervously Randy shifted from foot to foot. "My first song would be about the mighty Crow warriors of old."

"Ah, the old days," repeated Mr. Two Knives, shaking his head as he concentrated on his work.

"A song of thanks to the tree and deer for making the drum possible?" tried Randy.

Old Harry Two Knives rose, leaving the wood strips on his folding chair. "Maybe someday I'll remember how to make a drum." And he left.

Randy lay awake like a seething thunder cloud that night while his sister dreamed of victory in her dance tomorrow afternoon. What had Randy done wrong? Why wouldn't Two Knives teach him?

Before first light, the answer came to him. The old man *hadn't* said he wouldn't teach Randy. He simply left—and left the pieces of a drum on his chair.

Making frybread that morning, Randy's mother called, "Randy? Randy? Now where'd that boy get off to so early? He'll miss the Grand Opening Parade."

Following the flags (carried by veteran Crow soldiers) came five war chiefs with eagle feather war bonnets and beautiful beadwork costumes as they carried lance and bow on their great war horses. Behind them marched a great Crow nation—a thousand marching Crow all feeling lighter and taller marching in their traditional clothes and walking united.

Randy never gave the great spectacle a second thought. Alone in the dance pavilion since first light, Randy sat cross-legged in the grass with the wood pieces Two Knives had left for him. As he stared at the pieces, a vision came to him of a drum of perfect roundness making soothing sounds like the tapping of a thousand raindrops.

He fashioned the wood pieces before him into a roundness following that vision. Before he attached the drumhead, Randy picked up a stick and pretended to beat a gentle rhythm on the empty drum. In his mind he heard a song about the Creation of the Crow people. Randy closed his eyes and let his fingers beat the rhythm he heard on his empty drum.

When he finished, Randy noticed Harry Two Knives watching him. "That was a good song, Yellow Bear's son," said the old master, moving forward to inspect Randy's drum. "You have learned well the lessons of drum making. I will show you how to stretch the leather to make the sound of raindrops you heard. Then all living things can hear your song."

The Jingle Dress Competition was called. Hands sweating, knees trembling, Karla walked as steadily as she could to the center of the dance pavilion. So did 40 other girls.

"*Uta hey. Uta hey* [Let's go. Let's go]," called the master of ceremonies over the loud speakers.

Twenty drummers pounded on four giant drums to set a rhythm for the Jingle Dress dancers. The girls began to twirl and hop, arms flowing with the rhythm of their movements. Bells chimed like countless silver notes.

Randy, with his small drum, stepped to the edge of the grassy dance area. He closed his eyes and began to beat on his drum, a song of butterflies dancing over wildflowers, a song of rainbows after a soft summer rain, his song of creation.

The great drums and microphoned singers boomed over the stands and dancers at the dance pavilion. Randy's little drum seemed to be swallowed up by the mighty sound.

But not to Karla's feet. They seemed to hear the butterfly lightness of Randy's song. They hopped and pranced as only a butterfly can. Her bells jingled with a greater joy and lightness. On and on she danced as if floating on a rainbow. On and on he played, hardly aware that his hands were moving.

Both Karla and Randy felt the glory of the Crow Nation flow through them. Both tilted back their heads and yelped the joy cries of mighty Crow warriors, riding masters of the prairie. It was the Crow Fair and for these few days they were again the greatest people on earth!

FOR FURTHER READING

Here are a few good books to let you read more about the Crow Fair and the history of the Crow Nation.

Ancona, G. *Powwow*. San Diego, CA: Harcourt Paperbacks, 1998.

Crow, J. *From the Heart of the Crow Country: The Crow Indians' Own Stories*. Billings, MT: Bison Books, 2000.

Fitsgrald, M. *Yellowtail, Crow Medicine Man and Sun Dance Chief*. Norman, OK: University of Oklahoma Press, 1999.

Tarbescu, E. *The Crow*. New York: Franklin Watts, 2000.

Yellowtail, R. *Robert Summers Yellowtail at the Crow Fair*. Albuquerque, NM: Cold Type Services, 1993.

See your librarian for additional titles.

The Beat of a Dragon Boat
A Young Drummer Struggles to Find the Meaning of Winning

ABOUT THIS STORY

In cities all around the world on the fifth day of the fifth moon, great dragon-shaped boats are hauled into the water for races down rivers, across harbors, and through lakes. Some boats measure more than 100 feet in length (three school buses long) and can seat 70 rowers. The spectacular dragon-headed boats draw huge crowds to the dragon boat races that started in the Hunan province of China.

The festival started as a time set aside to remember and honor a brave and honorable man, Ch'u Yuan, who, more than 2,000 years ago, would not tolerate the corruption and greed of evil Prince Huai. He alone dared to openly protest the prince's dishonesty and wickedness. He was banished and, as a final protest against Huai's misuse of power, Ch'u Yuan threw himself into the Milo River and drowned.

Originally the boats did not race. But the ceremony of rowing to the spot where Ch'u Yuan drowned over the years became a great race. The boats, over the years, took on the look of dragons. Over the years, the races became famous and were staged in more and more locations around the world, so that now few remember that the festival is not about boat races, but about the memory of a noble statesman who would not accept corruption and injustice that hurt the common people of China.

The actions included in this story are accurate and typical of the mentioned events. The characters are fictional, but are based on actual events by real people.

The Beat of a Dragon Boat

On May 18, 1985, Chun Fang Hong rose even earlier than the sun and woke his six-year-old daughter, Yi Ching. His 14-year-old son, Mi Chan, was already up and stretching.

"Blessings of the Dragon Boat Festival, my children."

Mi Chan bolted for the door. "I still have work to do on our boat."

Fang Hong answered, "You are the drummer this year, my son. It is a great honor." After Mi Chan left, he added, "My heart would thrill to see his boat do well. But there are other boats with stronger crews. He is not even favored to finish in the top three."

At the river's edge Fang Hong and Yi Ching found Mi Chan busy with a dozen teammates waxing the hull of their sleek dragon boat. Over 90 feet long, thin, and fast, the boat would be rowed by 60 men. A fiery dragon head was carved into the wood at the front, standing twice as tall as any man. Its glowing black eyes glared ahead. Glossy red and green paint swept back from the head into wide stripes along the body of the boat and back to an equally ornate dragon tail at the stern, where a raised platform marked the spot where the drummer stood.

"Isn't it the most beautiful boat ever?" gushed Mi Chan. "And I know it's the fastest. This year we *have* to win!"

Fang Hong smiled and bowed his head.

The sun reached its peak, hot and fierce overhead. The people of Ying gathered by the riverbanks. Their festival clothes shone and sparkled with bright flashes of red, yellow, and blue. Rows of red flags flew in honor of Ch'u Yuan. The crowd buzzed with eager anticipation of the boat race.

One by one the great boats slid into the water, eight in all for this year's race. Three and four at a time, rowers stepped into the thin shells, paddles in hand, and took their seats. Each crew member wore bright bandannas and arm flags of the team's color. Last of all, the drummer waving long flags stepped into the stern of each boat. The crowd, along the bank, now thick as leaves on a fall forest floor, cheered loudly.

Mi Chan stood proudest of all as he tested his drum and shouted fierce victory cries to his rowers.

Fang Hong, with his wife and Yi Ching, stood near the starting line.

"Doesn't Mi Chan look splendid in his boat?"

A great gong sounded and the people cheered. It was time for the race. The boats glistened in the bright sunlight. Red flags waved along the shore. Gongs clanged.

Again the city's giant gong sounded and the boats were off! Muscles strained. Rowers yelled. Five hundred oars beat the green waters into foam. Eight great dragons lurched forward into their triumphant race down the river. Each drummer pounded his drum to set a rhythm for his boat's rowers. The crowd waved scarves and flags as they cheered.

Mi Chan strained to pound even harder on his drum as his boat fell into second and now back into third place. "Row!" he cried. "Row with all your heart!"

Mi Chan's boat slipped half a length, now a whole length behind as the people cheered for their favorites and ran along the bank to keep up, a moving sea of bright banners, flags, and scarves rippling along the shore.

"Faster! Faster!" cried Mi Chan, now in fourth place. More frenzied came his pounding on the boat's great kettledrum as he struggled to increase his rowers' speed.

"Row!" shouted Fang Hong.

"ROW!" shouted the crowd, sounding like the voice of a mighty dragon.

It flashed into Mi Chan's mind that he was going to lose. He could see that many of his rowers had stopped straining at their oars and rowed mechanically—just hard enough to get across the finish line. There was no way his boat could retake the lead, and no reason to struggle to try. The race was over for Mi Chan and his boat. Mi Chan's drumming became as mechanical as his rowers.

And then, completely unexpected and unlooked for, Mi Chan cocked his head, listening, as if a strange sound caught his soul. For a moment his mind forgot to tell his arms to pound. For a brief moment his mallets slowed.

"ROW!!" cried the crowd.

But Mi Chan was captured by a stirring, a calling from thousands of years away. Wide-eyed, he stared into the dazzling green water.

Then, as if waking from a dream, Mi Chan shook his head to clear his mind and squinted across the bright water at the now four other boats speeding ahead of his.

Embarrassed, Mi Chan frantically beat his drum. "This is the best boat and we will not give up! Row!" His voice rang with confidence, power, and authority that no one dared challenge.

The rowers cheered and again strained their backs and arms, redoubling the work of their paddles pulling against the calm green water.

"Row!" cried Mi Chan. "Row like the wind!"

As if lifted up by the dragon itself, Mi Chan's boat flew toward the finish.

At the finish line a great crowd cheered and waved. Mi Chan's boat sped across the line, nosing into second place.

The boats were pulled from the water. The crowds thinned back into Ying for feasting and music.

"You were far behind," said Mi Chan's father, his hands quietly tucked behind his back. "Yet you almost won. What happened?"

Mi Chan scrunched his eyebrows in confusion. "There was a moment when everyone in my boat could tell we were too far behind to win. We all seemed to accept that we were going to lose. Then, like in a dream, I could see Ch'u Yuan calling from the day he died. He *scolded* me for not doing what was right."

Mi Chan looked back at his gleaming boat and then again at his father. "Then I awoke and realized the right thing for us to do was to race as hard as we could whether or not we were going to win. I realized the right thing for me to do was to make my rowers *believe* they would win."

Fang Hong raised up a thin, bony hand and patted his son's shoulder, and a bright twinkle shone across his eyes. "Ch'u Yuan himself could not have drummed better. Today you were a mighty dragon, my son. Today you were better than the winner. You were your best."

Side by side, like mighty, swaggering dragons, father and son walked back into Ying to the smell of sweet rice cakes and the hot peppers cooking in woks for the evening meal. Laughing and dancing of the festival rang in their ears.

FOR FURTHER READING

Here are a few good books to let you read more about dragon boats and their place in Chinese history and culture.

Barker, P. *Dragon Boats: A Celebration*. London: Weatherhill, 1996.

Bouchard, D. *The Mermaid's Muse: The Legend of the Dragon Boats*. Vancouver, BC: Raincoast Books, 2002.

Chan, A. *Awakening the Dragon: The Dragon Boat Festival*. Montreal: Tundra Books, 2007.

Drumright, K. *Dog-Gone Dragon Boat*. Anchorage, AK: Windswept House, 1998.

Stepanchuk, C. *Red Eggs and Dragon Boats*. San Francisco: Pacific View Press, 1999.

See your librarian for additional titles.

Moans, Groans, and Bumps in the Dark
The Discovery of a *Real* Household Ghost

This story is extracted with publisher's permission from a story of the same name in *That's Weird! Awesome Science Mysteries* (Fulcrum, 2001). See *That's Weird! Awesome Science Mysteries* for the complete story and for additional references and follow-up activities.

ABOUT THIS STORY

Everyone enjoys a good ghost story. But *real* ghosts—spirits that walk around in your house, or your neighbors' house, and moan in the night—are different. Gallup Poll and other surveys show that more than one in four Americans believe that ghosts really exist. One in 14 claims to have personally encountered a ghost. That's more than 20,000,000 Americans who claim to have seen or heard a ghost!

This story combines the separate personal experiences of two friends of mine, both of whom have had very close and personal encounters with ghosts. Are the stories true? They both insist that they are. I know both people to be logical, rational people with advanced degrees and a healthy dose of scientific skepticism. So I believe them.

Moans, Groans, and Bumps in the Dark

The soggy, oven-like heat of a South Carolina August day was beginning to fade when the moving van pulled away and Pam Cocker wearily closed the front door on the frantic activity of moving-in day.

"Odd," she thought. Lazy Bones stood ridged in the hall facing the arched doorway into the dining room, hairs bristled all along her spine, lips curled back in the first ferocious growl of the dog's life. The thought that flashed across Pam's mind was that the dog looked more frightened than angry.

Pam Cocker had moved from New Jersey with her 10-year-old son, Tye, here to Spartanburg, South Carolina. Everything she owned had been crammed into a moving van and now was stuffed into this snug house with its grand sitting porch and beautiful shade trees.

Actually, only half of the load in the giant moving van had been Pam's. The other half belonged to a family moving from upstate New Jersey to somewhere in Alabama—not that Pam cared as long as her load was delivered first and on time.

"Odd," Pam thought again, after a dinner of delivered pizza, when the family cat, Withers—whom they called *Mr.* Withers—slowly backed away from the dining room and flattened himself against a wall, hissing venomously.

Next morning Pam began the chore of unpacking kitchen boxes and deciding into which cupboards, drawers, shelves, and nooks everything should go. Almost halfway through, she decided on a short break to sit on the back deck and watch Tye and Lazy Bones romp in the back yard.

She hadn't been outside 30 seconds when she heard a kitchen crash and then heard Mr. Withers spit and hiss in desperate fear and combat. She dashed inside to find every kitchen cupboard and drawer wide open and every item she had put away over the past two hours heaped in the middle of the floor. Every packing box had been dragged back into the dining room.

At first she blankly stared in shock and awe. Then her mind wondered ... *how*, trying to calculate how long it would have taken her to create such a mess. Then she wondered ... *who*, and her heart began to pound.

Pam screamed, "Who's there? Come out!"

She raced through the house carrying a carving knife. She heard not a sound and met not a soul. She couldn't think of anything to do but go back to unpacking.

By dinnertime they had unpacked three-quarters of their boxes and flopped onto the couch to watch TV and eat Chinese takeout. Lazy Bones and Mr. Withers lounged on the wall-to-wall carpet at their feet.

Bones' head snapped up. Then Mr. Withers sprang to his feet. Both animals growled at the empty, arched doorway into the dining room. As fiercely as they could, Bones and Withers hissed and barked at the doorway, slowly backing away as if being driven back by some great force.

Pam was frozen with a forkful of sesame chicken halfway to her mouth. Tye blinked as if he had missed something, his head slowly turning between the empty dining room doorway and the garage door through which the animals had fled.

Tye shuddered as a chilling breath of air blew across his arm and neck. "Must be the open garage door," he muttered and went back to dinner.

Pam wandered back downstairs before going to bed just to check the house and doors. Every packing box they had broken down that day was reassembled and stood in a great wall across the dining room.

Pam began to tremble. Her mind refused to accept that anything terrifyingly weird could happen—not to *her*.

But she also felt foolish as her mind flashed through pictures of ghosts and gremlins. She had a master's degree in science, for goodness' sake. She prided herself in her rational, problem-solving skills. There must be a logical explanation. Maybe she was just too tired to see it now.

Tye woke up in the pitch-black night, his heart pounding, his face bathed in a cold sweat. He had heard footsteps and his door opening. Hadn't he? Or was it just a dream? He settled back into a fitful sleep.

Sometime later the same sounds wove their way into a new dream. So did a touch, a cold, soft nudge on his arm, as if someone was trying to gain his attention.

No! That wasn't a dream. Tye jerked awake, gasping for breath. The room was empty. But the spot on his arm where he remembered being touched in his dream now burned as if it had been brushed by dry ice.

In the morning Pam found a slight burn—like frostbite—on Tye's arm where he had been touched. Other than for Lazy Bones and Mr. Withers being afraid to come out of the garage all day, that next day was uneventful.

During the darkest hours of the night, Pam awoke, hearing steps. She was about to check on Tye when her door opened. A vague, light-gray shadow shimmered in the doorway, the glowing outline of a man, dressed in rags that once had been elegant clothes. It—he—took a step forward to stand at the foot of her bed. Both terrified and fascinated, Pam realized that the ghost looked sad.

Pam thought she heard the word "home," like a low moan, full of despair and grief. Pam screamed for the thing to get out of her house and reached for her bedside light. The ghostly image was gone when light struck the room.

Downstairs all the packing boxes, which she'd broken down again, had been reassembled in the dining room.

In a flash of insight, Tye realized it wasn't the dining room or the house—it was the *moving boxes* the ghost seemed to be attached to. On a whim, Pam called the moving company and, making up the excuse that she thought she had one of their boxes, got the phone number of the family in Alabama whose furniture had shared the moving van.

A woman about Pam's age answered the phone. Pam introduced herself and asked if they had "lost" anything during the move.

For a long, awkward moment all Pam heard was the soft hiss of static on the line. The woman's voice seemed older and more tired when she said, "Oh. That's where Jefferson went."

"*Jefferson?*" Pam blurted. "The ghost has a name?! He's *your* ghost?"

The Alabama woman explained, "Jefferson was in our New Jersey house when we bought it. He popped out every month or so to rattle drawers—he loved to mess up kitchen and clothes drawers. We had hoped to leave him behind in NJ. That's why my husband took a new job and we moved."

The ghost had wanted to stay with his old family and had simply off-loaded at the wrong stop!

FOR FURTHER READING

Here are a few good books to let you read more about ghosts and research into their appearances.

Ballinger, E. *Monster Manual: A Complete Guide to Your Favorite Creatures.* Minneapolis, MN: Lerner, 1994.

Editors of *USA Weekend. I Never Believed in Ghosts Until ...* Chicago: Contemporary Books, 1992.

Hines, T. *Pseudoscience and the Paranormal.* New York: Prometheus Books, 1995.

Landau, E. *Ghosts.* Brookfield, CT: The Millbrook Press, 1995.

Randles, J., and P. Hough. *Encyclopedia of the Unexplained.* London: Michael O'Mara, Ltd., 1995.

Southhall, R. *How to Be a Ghost Hunter.* Woodbury, MN: Llewellyn Publications, 2003.

White, M. *Weird Science.* New York: Avon Books, 1999.

Wicks, C. *Ghost Tracks: What History, Science, and Fifty Years of Research Has Revealed about Ghosts.* New York: Author House, 2004.

Wilson, C. *Ghosts and the Supernatural.* New York: DK Publishing, 1995.

See your librarian for additional titles.

Shark Bait
Interns Face a Cruise to Tag Great White Sharks

This story is extracted with publisher's permission from a story of the same name in *Women at the Edge of Discovery* (Libraries Unlimited, 2003). See *Women at the Edge of Discovery* for the complete story and for additional references and follow-up activities.

ABOUT THIS STORY

Oceanographer Judith Bernard does her work in choppy northern California ocean waters infested with great white sharks. It is her job to lure the sharks close enough to tag and to collect tissue samples. How would you feel if you were trying to study a 25-foot-long monster shark as it circled closer and closer—studying you for its next meal?

The people and events mentioned in this story are real. Specific dialogue has been created for the story but is based on participants' reports and on interviews with them.

Shark Bait

The summer fog bank had receded a mile or more offshore when 38-year-old University of California biologist Judith

Bernard's 60-foot work boat, the *Jenny Mae*, muscled through the chop outside San Francisco's Golden Gate Bridge and veered north along the coast.

Two undergraduate summer interns had volunteered to assist with this shark-tagging expedition. One of them, 18-year-old Josh Landers, a marine economics major, asked, "Why study great whites? Why not just kill 'em?"

Judith snapped, "*We* should be learning from *them*. They are swimming computers that can sense light, sound, electrical fields, magnetic fields, and vibrations. They sense every creature within a half mile. Great whites have no fat, are almost totally disease free, and are one of only eight shark species that are warm blooded—and we don't know how they do it. We'd freeze. Besides they're highly intelligent. What better creature could there be to study?"

Josh folded his arms and shrugged. "One that doesn't want to eat me."

Nineteen-year-old biology sophomore Carol Martinez and Josh spent the last hour of their northward cruise mixing a smelly brew of tuna blood, fish guts, and crushed sardines. Then they ladled the smelly goo into the water off the stern diving platform, creating a tantalizing trail that led to the *Jenny Mae*.

Under Dr. Bernard's supervision, Carol prepared a box of barbed, oval marking tags. With luck, the interns would hook them into the dorsal fins of three or four sharks before the *Jenny Mae* headed home.

Tense and silent minutes followed while the boat inched forward on idle—all eyes waited eagerly, straining to see a dorsal fin cut through the rolling ocean swells. Both interns secretly hoped the man-eating monsters would never come near.

Carol cried, "Look! A fin!"

Judith ordered, "Toss out the rubber duck [a bright yellow float attached to the back half of a tuna and painted to look like a duck]."

Josh asked, "What's the duck for?"

"Great whites explore the world with their mouth. It's called test biting—sort of like picking up an unknown object with your hands to study it more closely. We don't know enough about this behavior."

"What's to know besides don't-let-it-happen-to-you?" Josh muttered.

Judith answered, "Great whites smell far better than humans. They can sense minute changes in electrical and magnetic fields through the water—even those caused by a human heartbeat. Their hearing is phenomenal. And yet for some reason they have to mouth things in order to understand them. And we don't know why. Watch."

The dorsal fin disappeared. The boat gently rocked with the steady swells.

"It's gone," Carol sighed.

"No. It's circling—studying us from below, spiraling in closer and closer."

Almost as if bored, the shark's snout eased out of the water. Even from 20 feet, the sight of this great predator was chilling. The tuna float was pulled into its gaping mouth. The shark held for a second and let go. Again it seized the float, shook lightly, and again let go, sinking out of sight into the blue. It hadn't eaten the tuna, but left great rips where its serrated teeth sawed through the meat.

"See?" said Judith. "It was only testing the float."

Josh stammered, "But that could have been my leg!"

Judith nodded. "Yes. That's what happens to most humans who are attacked. Great whites test bite and let go. If a great white was really after you, you'd never live to tell the tale." She called to a deck hand, "Drag the tuna to the stern. We'll try to get the shark to come close."

"You want the shark *closer?*" gasped Josh.

Judith directed Josh to climb onto the diving platform, a wooden ledge behind the stern railing. The platform ran the width of the boat, was three feet wide, and rested six inches above the waterline.

The shark cruised past the stern of the *Jenny Mae.*

"A five-meter female," Judith announced, squinting down at the dark silhouette now drifting a few feet under the surface in a counterclockwise circle around the boat. It looked like the shadow of a passing cloud. Judith tossed a new hunk of tuna into its path, hoping to lure the shark to the surface. It looped past, ignoring the bait.

"Look. It's already been tagged," called Josh.

The shark rose to nudge the tuna with its snout. Kneeling less than four feet away on the platform, Josh called out scars, markings, and approximate age.

And then the tuna was gone, almost like a magician's trick. In the blink of an eye the shark sucked it under and down its gullet.

Judith said, "Splash your hand in the water."

"Do *what?*" cried Josh. "The shark's still down there!"

Judith explained, "We have to draw it closer if I'm to study how a great white explores its world."

"Yeah. Like how it eats," added Josh, staring at his hand and the rippling ocean surface.

"It knows your hand is there. No human can touch the ocean without some shark sensing it."

Judith stared past the sunlight dancing off the surface into the dark waters below. A deep, expectant quiet settled over the *Jenny Mae*, broken only by the soft lapping of the swells against the hull and the light splash of Josh's fingers.

The water under Josh's hand seemed to bulge slightly. Reflexively, he jerked his hand up just as the snout and gaping mouth of this 16-foot, three-ton predator broke vertically through the surface of the ocean, like a slow-motion submarine-launched missile, and hung there for a moment only two feet from his face as if wondering where the hand had gone.

Water streamed off its snout and gurgled from its mouth as it rose higher. The snout was deeply scarred—perhaps from test biting too many shark cages and boat motor mounts. The mouth was still bloody from its last feast. The finger-long serrated teeth almost glowed pearl white against pink gums.

Smiling, Judith said, "See? Great whites are really very curious and playful."

"*Playful?!*" Carol blurted. "It tried to eat Josh!"

Judith climbed onto the dive platform beside Josh and instructed, "Hand me the tissue pole [an eight-foot metal pole with an "O"-shaped surgical blade on the end to punch out a small core sample of tissue and blood]."

Judith knelt on the dive platform holding the tissue pole like a harpoon. The shark seemed to wander away, then wheeled on its right pectoral fin and glided back toward the boat. It paused and rose out of the water, treading water with its tail while one black eye stared at the boat. Then it flopped forward as if to say, "Put your hand back in my ocean. I'm ready to play again."

"Did you *see* that?" Carol exclaimed. "That was … weird."

Judith answered, "It's called spyhopping. Quite normal for great whites. They do it mostly to search for seals." Again she focused on the shark. "Come on back, girl…. A little closer …"

The dark shadow of the shark knifed toward the diving platform. In a lightning-quick strike, Judith jabbed her pole forward. Before the shark could react, the pole was back out of the water and Judith was transferring the tissue sample into a glass test tube for shipment to the lab.

Judith called to a deck hand, "Bring out the shark cage. We're going in."

"We're gonna *swim* … in the *water?* … With the *shark?*" Josh stammered, suddenly thinking that marine sciences was a bad choice of majors.

FOR FURTHER READING

Here are a few good books to let you read more about great white sharks.

Arnold, C. *Watch Out for Sharks!* New York: Clarion Books, 1997.
Berger, G. *Sharks.* Garden City, NY: Doubleday, 1994.

Cerullo, M. *The Truth about Great White Sharks*. Minneapolis, MN: Lerner Publishing, 2001.

Ellis, R. *Great White Shark*. Palo Alto, CA: Stanford University Press, 1999.

Klimley, P., ed. *Great White Sharks*. Burlington, MA: Academic Press, 1998.

Lawrence, R. D. *Shark! Nature's Masterpiece*. Shelbury, VT: Chapter Publishers, 1994.

Markle, Sandra. *Outside and inside Sharks*. New York: Atheneum Books for Young Readers, 1996.

Peschak, T. *South Africa's Great White Shark*. London: Struik, 2007.

Romashko, Sandra. *Shark: Lord of the Sea*. Miami, FL: Windward Publications, 1994.

See your librarian for additional titles.

A Name at the Dance
A Boy Fears Ridicule and Scorn during the Naming Dance

ABOUT THIS STORY

Each of the southeastern American tribes (Creek, Choctaw, Chickasaw, Cherokee, Timucua, and Calusa) has always held a major ceremony as the new corn crop ripened. These are not typical harvest festivals held after harvest has been completed. Rather, the Green Corn Festival is held as corn first ripens, ready for picking, but before even one ear has been picked and eaten.

These Green Corn Festivals have served several important purposes besides giving thanks for a successful harvest to come. They have acted, in effect, as new year celebrations, since the tribal year is marked from one Green Corn Festival to the next. They served as the annual principal opportunity for the conduct of tribal business. Finally they served a spiritual purpose. The Green Corn Festival was a time for each individual to purify him- or herself, to seek and bestow forgiveness, and to reestablish harmony within the tribe.

As tribes have integrated into American life, much of the importance of festivals has been lost. Business is now conducted by phone, fax, and e-mail. Meetings are only a few hours' flight away. Spirituality is handled through the practice of weekly religious services. Unemployment and economic pressures have changed tribal attitudes toward traditional celebrations. Still, the annual festival and its many ceremonies continue to be critically important to the tribe. Certainly this is true for new 12-year-olds facing the Naming Dance at each year's festival.

The events included in this story are accurate and typical of the mentioned events. The characters are fictional, but are based on actual events by real people.

A Name at the Dance

One step forward, one step back. Hop-turn. Hop-turn. Shuffle …

"What are you doing?"

"Go away. I'm practicing."

Eleven-year-old Myron Osceola stood in the doorway watching his friend Billy Wingfeet kick up dust in the long council ceremonial lodge. A thick streak of heat and sunlight stabbed into the cool, dark interior of the lodge through the open doorway. With everyone else in the tribe outside watching the Seminole nation chief say the prayers of thanks to open the annual Green Corn Festival for 1972, the lodge stood empty.

"I'm 12," said Billy. "It's my year to be named. But I don't have the steps right for the Naming Dance."

"*That* was the Naming Dance?" guffawed Myron.

Billy grunted. Myron would never have to worry about what name the council gave him next year. *He* was a natural dancer.

"Your rhythm is all wrong," added Myron. "Dance the Naming Dance that way and they'll name you Leadfoot."

"It's not funny! The name they give me will be a part of me for all my life."

The lodge, like the surrounding Seminole chickees (houses), was built of Cypress poles with interwoven palmetto fronds. Over 80 feet long, the lodge had two flap-covered entrances—the women's entrance at the northeast corner and the men's at the southwest, where Myron now stood. Four long rows of wooden benches, raised like mini-bleachers, stood against the north and south walls. Unraised rows of low, backless benches were stacked against the shorter east and west walls.

"Don't worry so much," said Myron. "Or they'll name you Black Cloud."

"I said, no name jokes!" snapped Billy.

Billy Wingfeet returned to his halting practice. *One step forward, one step back. Hop-turn. Hop-turn.* "Don't stand there gawking. Either go play or help."

One hour later, dripping sweat on this muggy August afternoon in the Big Cypress Swamp Seminole Reservation in southern Florida, the two friends threw back the cover flap and stepped outside into the happy atmosphere of a festival, an important council meeting, and a family reunion.

Scattered from Florida to Oklahoma, the Seminole tribe gathers each year at the Big Cypress Swamp Seminole Reservation for the Green Corn Festival. Over 800 had gathered in this year of 1972, crowded into domed clan chickees fanned out from the council's ceremonial lodge.

A great crowd of Seminole from the three Florida reservations watched as a shaman lit a new fire and gave thanks. The spark caught, spreading into flame. The flame fanned into fire, the first of the new year. All fires on the reservation had been put out early that morning to mark the end of another year. Now a new fire had been lit, a new beginning, a pure fire to symbolize a renewed purity for the people.

"Come on. Let's play ball," begged Myron.

"You go ahead," replied Billy. Billy Wingfeet could not concentrate on ball games or even on the meaning of the festival. *One step forward, one step back. Hop-turn. Hop-turn.* Tomorrow he would be given his tribal name!

As the chief's opening finished, burning coals were carried to each chickee. The shaman carried a flame inside the lodge to relight the council fire. Fires blazed in the shimmering summer heat and festival cooking began. Mounds of corn were roasted and boiled, alligator and beef were roasted for stews, sofki (a mashed corn drink) was passed in tall glasses to the men who had fasted in preparation for the dances of the Green Corn Festival. Pots of squash and swamp cabbage were heated and stirred.

As the sun set, fiery red over the western swamp, the drums and rattles began to play. "Billy!" called his mother. "Come and eat before the Stomp Dances."

Billy shrugged. How could he eat when tomorrow was such an important day, and when he still feared his clan would be shamed by his dancing?

Rather than watch the twirling dancers with their rattles and elaborate head dresses and costumes, rather than sit with his family and clan and listen to the driving beat of the many pounding drums, Billy sat alone and cross-legged in his mother's chickee.

He sat and he prayed and he concentrated as he had seen his uncles do. He no longer tried to picture each individual step of the Naming Dance; now he tried to picture himself with winged feet flying, soaring across the dance floor, tried to picture smiles and nods of approval on every face on the council and in the watching crowd.

But try as he might, Billy didn't think it was working. He still felt like Billy Leadfoot.

When Billy awoke in the morning, council meetings had already started. Only three hours to the Naming Dance. There were only 11 12-year-olds this year for everyone to watch. He would never be able to hide in the middle of a dancing crowd.

One step forward, one step back. Hop-turn. Hop-turn. Again he tried to picture the steps in his mind and to send the image to his feet.

In what felt like a blink the Naming Dance was announced. The 12-year-olds were summoned. Billy's heart pounded against his ribs. He didn't dare look at any of his clan members or at the other dancers as he stood in the middle of the lodge, waiting. The shaman said prayers for these 11 youngsters who were about to join the tribe as adults and explained the importance of the names they would be given by the council.

Quit talking and let us get it over with! shouted Billy inside his head.

The drums began to pound. The rhythm seemed to beat inside Billy's chest and calm his heart. The jangling rattles seemed to lift his troubled spirits.

One step forward, one step back. Hop-turn. Hop-turn.

Eyes squeezed closed, Billy began to dance. He started at the northeast corner of the open lodge floor to honor his mother and her clan. He danced to the southwest to pay respect to his father.

One step forward, one step back. Hop-turn. Hop-turn.

With surprise, almost with shock, Billy realized that he felt *good* dancing. He cracked open one eye to see if his clan were laughing or turning away in shame.

No! They were nodding approval. Myron cheered from a thicket of watchers on the benches of the lodge's west end. Even Billy's mother and uncles smiled and clapped!

Now Billy felt like a Wingfeet! He sprang into the middle of the dancers feeling like his feet really had sprouted wings. His arms flew with wild triumph; his body and heart soared.

The council elders nodded in recognition and smiled. Another Wingfeet had earned his name. They had known he would. His clan had always been good dancers. A good harvest, good dances, good meetings. It would be another good year.

FOR FURTHER READING

Here are a few good books to let you read more about the Green Corn Festival and about the Seminole tribe.

Downs, D. *Patchwork: Seminole Art and Activities.* Sarasota, FL: Pineapple Press, 2005.

Franco, E. *The Green Corn Festival.* New York: Voluntad, 1999.

Jumper, B. *Legends of the Seminole.* Sarasota, FL: Pineapple Press, 1998.

MacCauley, C. *The Seminole Indians of Florida.* New York: Kessinger Publishing, 2006.

Miller, J. *American Indian Festivals.* Chicago: Children's Press, 1997.

Sonneborn, L. *The Seminole.* New York: Franklin Watts, 2002.

Takacs, S. *The Seminole.* Chicago: Children's Press, 2004.

See your librarian for additional titles.

Holi!
Two Boys Enjoy a Celebration of India

This story is extracted with publisher's permission from a story of the same name in *New Years to Kwanzaa* (Fulcrum, 1999). See *New Years to Kwanzaa* for the complete story and for additional references and follow-up activities.

ABOUT THIS STORY

Holi is unique among the celebrations of the world. Partly it is an agricultural festival celebrating the winter harvest in northern India. Partly it is a spring festival, marking the passage of seasons and of the year. Partly, Holi is a religious celebration, honoring the triumph of good over evil, and the victories of the Lord Krishna. But Holi is also a time of planned and sanctioned madness, a time of public wildness.

On the day of Holi, colored powder may be sprayed, and colored water may be squirted or thrown in water balloons onto anyone—anytime! And no one gets angry. No one grows resentful. It is Holi!

The events included in this story are accurate and typical of the mentioned events. The characters are fictional, but are based on actual events by real people.

Holi!

"I'm giving you *lots* of wood this year. So no Holi tricks. No squirt-ing." Mr. Sahir stood at the door of his whitewashed one-story house in the town of Pharenda, northern India. A late afternoon sun blazed fire-red down the street, making his deep-set green eyes glow more fiercely and suspicious in the doorway. A light breeze flowed through his thin cotton shirt and pants to cool his skin this warm March.

Both Kavi and Rajak blinked innocently. "No, Mr. Sahir. We won't trick you on Holi this year." With dirty faces, loose-fitting white pants, white linen shirts, and broad smiles, both boys stepped forward to wrestle the wood outside.

Kavi and Rajak were two of hundreds of children scrounging wood for the great Holi fires. As they dragged their load down the wind-ing dirt street toward a great town clearing at the river, Kavi and Rajak stopped next to a cluster of bushes.

"Do you have the bamboo blowpipes?" asked Kavi.

"And the yellow and red powders," answered Rajak, pointing at their secret stash hidden beneath the bush.

"I've got the water balloons."

"We're ready for Holi!" And both boys laughed. "Watch out, Mr. Sahir!"

The sun hung like an orange ball on the hills through the haze to the west. "Hurry," said Kavi. "The moon's going to rise. We've got to get our wood to the bonfire."

A full moon was due to rise this evening of March 25. That meant tomorrow was Holi. Tonight would be a night of magic fol-lowed by a day of wild fun.

A great crowd buzzed around the mound of wood, paper, discarded furniture and crates, and torn straw and baskets. Friends and neighbors laughed together. Music played from a hundred instruments carried to the river clearing.

Kavi and Rajak added their load of wood to the great mound just as the sun disappeared in a fiery blaze in the west and a golden full moon rose in the east over the low hills of the jungle. The night blew warm and friendly. The heat and mugginess of the monsoons were still a month away.

With rounds of applause, burning torches were brought forward and soon the great Holi bonfire blazed hot and bright. People laughed and cheered. Sticks of sugarcane were passed to the children.

People sang. Clusters of young women with large, almond-shaped eyes began folk dances around the fire.

Kavi and Rajak sat with their families watching the pulsing glow of the flames and the dense smoke billow into the spring night to turn the rising moon a deep red. Music floated up with the rising heat from a dozen impromptu groups around the fire. Elders told Holi myths and stories.

After each story the crowd cheered, and music erupted from drums, horns, and stringed instruments around the great fire. People sang, danced, and laughed. The glowing full moon poured down its light. It was a night of radiant magic.

One by one, families drifted off to home and sleep as the bonfire faded to glowing red embers.

When the sun climbed hot and clear over Pharenda next morning, families drifted back to the bonfire clearing. Each person dipped a finger into the warm ashes and marked their forehead to wish for luck in the coming year.

Then the fun of Holi began!

Kavi and Rajak dashed away from the bonfire clearing, the first red rays of morning lighting their faces, and stopped next to the bush with their stash of Holi weapons.

"Soon we'll make *everyone* see red," laughed Kavi, snatching up a two-foot long bamboo blowpipe and bags of red and yellow powder.

"Especially Mr. Sahir!" said Rajak, filling three balloons with yellow water.

But Mr. Sahir was already hurrying through the maze of narrow streets toward his shop.

"There he goes," cried Kavi. "He's ahead of us."

"Through this alley. We'll cut him off," answered Rajak, already sprinting through a narrow gate opening.

The boys heard, "Balloons away!" and glanced up as two water balloons plummeted on them from above.

One exploded in the alley right in front of Kavi, spraying red water across his pants and bare feet. The other, a perfect shot, crashed into Rajak's upturned face, soaking him with saffron-stained yellow water.

"Holi!" cried the laughing children from above.

"Fire back!" cried Rajak.

The boys launched two water balloons that exploded against the roof tiles above them. But both attackers were already gone, off to seek new targets.

"Quick. After Mr. Sahir," ordered Kavi.

Mr. Sahir rounded the corner and stepped toward his linen shop. Kavi whispered, "Blowpipes," and both boys poured generous amounts of colored powder into one end of their pipes.

With a soft "Now!" the boys sprang into the street and blew out their yellow billows at Mr. Sahir.

"Holi!"

A saffron yellow cloud enveloped Mr. Sahir. He ducked. He turned. He screamed. But he could not escape the dust of Holi.

"But you promised!" bellowed Mr. Sahir, wiping saffron powder from his eyes and teeth.

"Balloons!" cried Rajak. Splat! A red water balloon exploded across Mr. Sahir's shoulder.

"Promises never count on Holi!" Both boys dashed down the street, laughing—and straight into a great cloud of colored powder blown by three girls. "Holi!!"

No one wore good clothes on Holi. The boys fired their last two full water balloons. One sailed high and splattered red across a house. One hit square into the back of one of the girls. She staggered for a step under the explosion of bright yellow water.

Kavi and Rajak chased the girls two blocks before they walked into another red and yellow ambush. "Holi! Holi!"

By noon Kavi and Rajak were out of powder and balloons, and were painted head to toe in bright red and yellow. So were most other children in Pharenda. So were many adults.

The boys parted, each toward his own home and the family feasts that would mark the end of Holi.

The food was plentiful and succulent. But it was the cries of "Holi!" and the perfectly timed attacks with powder and water balloon that would linger longest in the boys' memory.

FOR FURTHER READING

Here are a few good books to let you read more about Holi and other celebrations of India.

Bennett, O. *Holi*. London: Hamish Hamilton, Ltd., 1997.
Jones, M. *Divali and Holi*. New York: Scholastic, 2004.
Kadodwala, D. *Holi*. London: Evans Brothers, 2004.
Krishnaswam, U. *Holi*. Chicago: Children's Press, 2003.
Manchanda, S. *Holi*. Columbia, MO: South Asia Books, 1999.
Pandya, M. *Here Comes Holi: The Festival of Colors*. Wellesley, MA: MeeRa Publications, 2003.

See your librarian for additional titles.

The Tiger Attacks
A Boy's Experience of the Chinese Kite-Flying Wars

This story is extracted with publisher's permission from a story of the same name in *New Years to Kwanzaa* (Fulcrum, 1999). See *New Years to Kwanzaa* for the complete story and for additional references and follow-up activities.

ABOUT THIS STORY

Some celebrations are conducted in greatest seriousness. Some seem a mere excuse for fun and play. Ch'ung Yeung Chieh (the Chinese kite-flying ceremony) looks like one of the latter. However, Ch'ung Yeung Chieh commemorates, and reenacts, a most serious and sad event in Chinese history.

To watch Ch'ung Yeung Chieh is to watch families swarm to the tops of high hills and spend the day flying kites. These are not ordinary kites. These are elaborate, giant kites painted in a rainbow of the brightest colors and fashioned into every imaginable shape. Many are built with wires, tubes, and even flutes and gourds to hum, whistle, wail, blow, and chime while they fly.

Beyond displaying their kites, each flyer is engaged in aerial combat. Ch'ung Yeung Chieh is a day of kite wars! Last kite flying is the winner. All who watch or participate spend a delightful day. And maybe, during the excitement and fun, some remember the 2,000-year-old tragedy that started the celebration.

The events included in this story are accurate and typical of the mentioned events. The characters are fictional, but are based on actual events by real people.

The Tiger Attacks

Tsuan Chou Chi eagerly greeted his eight-year-old son, Kam Hong, at first light in the family's small cinderblock house on the outskirts of Foochow, China. Outside a crisp, clear morning was emerging this October 3, 1987.

"The ninth day of the ninth moon. The day of Ch'ung Yeung Chieh."

Chou Chi carried a monstrous, paper, winged tiger from the back room. Sharp claws and fangs of glittering red streamers trailed off one side. The eyes were the color of glowing jade. The body was painted curving stripes of yellow, orange, and black. The wings were iridescent red.

"Oh, my!" breathed Kam. "It's a magnificent tiger, father." Kam feared if he reached forward to touch the beast it would snap his hand off, so fierce and real it looked.

"Look here," directed Chou Chi, holding the kite over his head and pointing to five bamboo tubes he had tied into the string rigging underneath. "These will howl like a tiger on the prowl once they catch the wind! This tiger might just *frighten* the other kites out of the sky."

Carrying the tiger and picnic, the family joined the long line marching to the top of Fei-fang Hill, one of the highest of the grassy hills surrounding Foochow. The top offers a breathtaking view of Foochow, the winding Minjiang River valley, and even the East China Sea far off to the east.

Each family carried a huge kite—some shaped like owls, some like turtles or dragons, some like giant boxes, some like giant fish, some like birds or butterflies.

The sky above Fei-fang Hill was already full of frogs, centipedes, dragons, owls, and birds. An eerie wail from noise-makers attached to the kites floated across the crowd, who eagerly watched as kites dipped and climbed in the stiff breeze.

Wearing gloves to protect his hands, Kam held the string while Chou Chi raised the mighty tiger over his head and angled it into the wind. The bamboo tubes began to moan, the wings to flutter, and Kam's tiger leapt into the air. Streamer claws and fangs snapped in the wind as the tiger climbed hungrily into the crowded sky.

The crowd pointed and cheered at the new tiger. Then they gasped as an enormous box kite took to the air, so big it took four men to control the strings and keep it from flying away. As big as a small house, the red and yellow monster box seemed to crash straight through smaller kites as it muscled its way into the sky.

"Stay away from that one, Kam Hong," warned Chou Chi. "It could tear our tiger to pieces."

And so the kite wars began.

Flyers tried to maneuver their kite to cross strings with another kite. Then the flyer would pull and vibrate his string to cut the string of the opponent's kite. It takes great skill to cut through a kite string in this way. Some flyers worked their kites high into the sky and then pulled them into a steep nose dive, crashing straight down onto another unsuspecting kite and knocking it from the sky.

Kam banked his tiger to the left and crossed strings with a rainbow-bright owl. With quick, jerking tugs, Kam sawed his kite string against the owl's.

The owl's flyer tried to bank left and escape. Kam banked with him, still sawing, until with a sharp snap, the owl broke loose from its flyer's string and fluttered to the ground.

Kam's tiger roared and swooped right, searching for another victim.

"There's a dragon below and to your right," cried Chou Chi. "Get him!"

Kam pulled on his kite string. The tiger roared across the sky and crossed strings with a fearsome-looking dragon. Both flyers jerked on their strings, trying to cut the other's line.

"Watch out for the box kite!" cried Chou Chi.

The monstrous box kite lumbered through the air and crossed strings with Kam. The box's four thick control strings seemed to surround Kam's one.

Kam's tiger was trapped between the dragon's string on one side and the giant box's lines on the other.

"Slide out! Escape!" yelled Chou Chi.

Kam curved his tiger kite hard against the dragon's string and pulled with all his might. Snap! The dragon's string broke. Kam yanked hard the other way. His tiger dove left and curved away from the giant box.

The four-person box kite team also pulled hard left, following Kam's fleeing tiger. Kam pulled right and dipped his tiger into a dive. The box tried to follow but lost its hold on the wind and fluttered, momentarily helpless in the sky.

Kam had escaped.

The crowd cheered its approval of his maneuver.

The day wore on. Fewer and fewer kites soared through the gusty winds. The sun circled around the hill to cast the kites' long shadows across Foochow below. Kam's father fed him the special *teng-kao* cakes his mother had made for their picnic. These cakes were made of sticky rice pastry filled with spiced meats and fruits and then steamed.

The cakes warmed Kam's stomach and eased the ache in his arms from struggling against tiger and wind all day.

Then Kam saw an opportunity. The great box was attacking a fish kite. Kam swooped his line across two of the box's control strings and began to jerk his line to cut through those strings. Just as the fish's line snapped, so did two of the box's four lines.

The mammoth box lurched to the right and shuddered in the sky as its team of flyers struggled to compensate for the loss of two strings. Kam's tiger dipped right and attacked a third of the box's strings.

Snap! Before the box flyers could regain control, that third string broke under the attack of Kam's mighty tiger.

The box fluttered out of control and, like a wounded duck, sank to the ground.

The crowd roared. Kam's tiger soared into the sky, roaring through its bamboo voice.

"Well done, Kam!" cheered his father. "With the great box gone you will triumph for sure."

A fight high in the sky between a caterpillar and a butterfly sent the losing butterfly spiraling toward the ground far below.

Crash! The butterfly smashed straight down onto Kam's tiger, snapping the wood supports for one wing. The wounded tiger hung in the air for a moment as if clawing to hold onto the sky. Then, its back and wing broken, it sank with a final eerie moan to the grass.

Kam froze, unable to believe his eyes as he stared at his fallen champion.

His father chuckled, "That is the way of things. The tiger rules the heavens one minute and is brought down by the flutter of a butterfly the next."

Chou Chi lifted his son's chin to ward off any tears. "You were a magnificent kite flyer today, Kam Hong. I couldn't be prouder of you. This has been a glorious day. Come, let's salute the kites that remain in the air and head for home."

As the family carried their broken tiger and empty picnic basket down Fei-fang Hill, Kam added, "And we have a whole year to make our tiger even better!"

FOR FURTHER READING

Here are a few good books to let you read more about the Chinese Kite-Flying Celebration and about other Chinese annual celebrations.

Chongquing Editorial Staff. *The Traditional Chinese Festivals and Tales*. Hong Kong: Chongquing Publishing House, 2002.

Chungen, L. *Chinese Kites*. Sydney, Australia: Foreign Language Press, 2000.

Goh, P. *Origins of Chinese Festivals*. San Jose, CA: Asiapac Books, 2005.

Wei, L. *Legends of Ten Chinese Festivals*. Key Largo, FL: Dolphin Books, 2002.

Wong, C. *Mooncakes and Hungry Ghosts: Festivals in China*. South San Francisco, CA: China Books and Periodicals, 1999.

Zhu, J. *Chinese Traditions and Festivals*. Aberdeen, SD: Evergreen Publishing, 1998.

See your librarian for additional titles.

Stories from the Natural World

Slithering Strikes
A Boy's Encounter with a Cobra

This story is extracted with publisher's permission from a story of the same name in *Close Encounters with Deadly Dangers* (Libraries Unlimited, 1999). See *Close Encounters with Deadly Dangers* for the complete story and for additional references and follow-up activities.

ABOUT THIS STORY

Humans have always been fascinated by poisonous snakes. Cobras, especially, hold a special spot in our nightmares and darkest dreams. Cobras, however, are far from the most poisonous of snakes. Bushmasters, black mambas, and sea snakes, for example, are far deadlier.

Cobras seem magical because of the way they look at us before they strike. Other snakes coil and strike. Only cobras raise their heads high in the air like waving vines or thin tree trunks. Only cobras spread an evil-looking hood at the back of their head before they attack. Only cobras hiss, sounding like one human "shhhhhh-ing" another. Only cobras dance in the marketplace, waving their hooded heads three or four feet in the air at the command of a snake charmer's flute. Cobras are unique among snakes.

Cobras are also the most dangerous snake to humans. Cobras kill more people each year (thousands in China and India alone) than any other snake species. Virtually every one of those deaths occurs at night. The cobra is a nocturnal hunter, slithering through the grass when you can't even see it coming.

The events included in this story represent normal, prototypical behavior for each species mentioned. The actions and events in the story happen many times each year in the wild.

Slithering Strikes

I lay on a rock outcropping, my father's rifle at my side, waiting to shoot the wild pigs that had been eating our family's vegetable garden. It was night and I fought constantly to stay awake, waiting for the pigs to return.

My name is Ishani. I am 16. My family owns a sugarcane farm in the Kerela District along the southern coast of India. Farms climb the steep hills behind the wide beaches where patches of jungle have been cleared away. Our sugarcane field is one of these farms.

A full moon hung in the sky. Colors were all soft grays. But the strong moonlight cast the outline of every object clear and crisp.

I heard the distant, soft grunts of pigs and tensed.

I also heard a soft rustling through the grass next to my blanket.

It must be a mouse come to sneak a nibble of my sandwich, I thought. I would have kicked at the mouse, but the grunts were coming closer, and I didn't want to alert the pigs to my presence.

The pigs trotted into my view, casting hard shadows along the narrow path, a mother and three babies. Slowly, silently, my hand tightened its grip on my father's rifle. I raised it from the blanket.

I realized the nearby rustling was too long, too big to be a mouse or rat. It sounded more like … like a snake quietly slithering through the dried grass. I remembered that a cobra had been spotted near here a few weeks ago.

The grunting pigs were below me. But the rustling was *very* close.

I froze, rifle held in mid-air. It *was* a snake, a *big* snake. I could see the soft bands of color on its back in the moonlight. A cobra! I heard the soft flicking of its tongue. My heart pounded so loudly I was sure the snake could hear.

My mind knew that cobras strike at movement. I would be safer if I stayed absolutely still. But my feet didn't believe it. They wanted to run.

I heard the snake slither cautiously onto my blanket. I felt its dry skin slide across my bare knee and under the other leg. Eyes squeezed shut, I struggled to suppress a violent shudder. My legs desperately wanted to jump away, kicking wildly at the dreaded snake. I could feel its powerful muscles contract as its skin undulated across my leg.

The cobra seemed to take hours to creep across my legs, and felt like it must be 50 feet long. All snakes are cold blooded, but this cobra's skin felt warm against my legs as if it had been basking on hot rocks all day.

I heard the soft plop of the cobra's tail as it dropped past my leg and onto my blanket. The pigs were forgotten. I wanted only to get back to the safety of our family home. As soon as the cobra disappeared into the tall grass, I ran.

I scrambled into one of the wide gullies I'd have to cross to get back home. I didn't care how much noise I made, as long as I reached the safety of our house and stopped shivering.

Then I heard the rustling behind me, like a soft whisper through the undergrowth. I saw the dry grasses rhythmically wave as something passed invisibly along the ground.

The cobra!

I froze again, pressing my back into the dark shadows along the soft dirt side of the gully. My stomach began to churn and my knees grew weak.

Ten feet from me the cobra stopped. Majestically it raised its head and upper body, three feet, four feet, almost five feet in the air! Its head gently swayed as its shiny, black eyes and flicking tongue surveyed me. I could feel it stare at me and remembered that a cobra's night vision is far better than mine. In terror I realized this cobra stood taller than I did.

I knew it couldn't strike from there. Cobras don't *spring* forward, and so can only strike as far forward as they have raised their head off the ground.

The cobra dropped back to the grass with a sharp plop. Almost before I could blink, its head rose again above the grass. It was closer this time. Close enough to strike, close enough for me to touch it if I stretched out my arm. I stared at the gently waving head, almost too frightened to breathe.

The cobra slowly spread its hood. I used to think it was just loose skin a cobra spread into the famous wide, flat hood at the back of its head. My father says it is actually a set of ribs the cobra can raise and flatten to push the skin out into a hood. My mother says cobras do it to frighten their victims. It worked. I was *terrified*. Especially when I remembered that cobras form a hood just before they strike.

My father's rifle was still in my hand. But I knew it was useless. Even if I had the gun raised and aimed, the cobra might well strike faster than I could squeeze the trigger.

Then the cobra began to hiss. Actually, it sounded very much like the sharp "Shhhhh!" one person might hiss at another to quiet them in a movie theater.

With deep dread I remembered that a hiss is the last thing a cobra does before it lunges at its victim.

I don't remember where the mongoose came from. I don't know whose mongoose it was. It must have been sitting on the dirt bank above me. But faster than either the cobra or I could see, it raced past me and latched onto the cobra's neck.

That mongoose saved my life when nothing else in the world could have. Before the cobra could change targets and lash forward with its deadly poison, the mongoose was at its throat, gripping the cobra's neck with all four feet. The mongoose savagely bit the cheek and lower jaw of the cobra. Then it darted back, stopping five or six feet from the cobra, panting to catch its breath. The whole attack lasted only three or four seconds.

As the cobra raised its wounded head, hissing in anger, the mongoose scampered in for a second time. Again it grabbed onto the cobra's neck and nipped and bit at its cheek, neck, and lower jaw. Again it sped back to safety to catch its breath.

Three times, four times, five, the mongoose fearlessly raced in a lightning blur to attack this dreaded cobra many times its size. It moved and struck faster than I could see in the yellow moonlight.

In less time than the cobra's venom would have killed *me*, the cobra lay dead in the dry grass of the gully and my hero mongoose had scampered off.

Still shaking and dazed, I coiled the 40-pound cobra body over my shoulders and scrambled up the bank toward home.

FOR FURTHER READING

Here are a few good books to let you read more about cobras and mongooses.

Ethan, E. *Cobras*. Milwaukee, WI: Gareth Stevens Publications, 1995.

Johnson, S. *Cobras*. Minneapolis, MN: Lerner Publications, 2006.

Lockwood, S. *Cobras: The World of Reptiles*. Mankato, MN: Child's World, 2006.

Mara, W. *Venomous Snakes of the World*. Neptune, NJ: T.F.H. Publications, 1993.

Wallach, V. *Uncover a Cobra*. Sarasota, FL: Silver Dolphin Books, 2005.

See your librarian for additional titles.

A "Croc" of Jaws
A Young Crocodile's First Attack

This story is extracted with publisher's permission from a story of the same name in *Close Encounters with Deadly Dangers* (Libraries Unlimited, 1999). See *Close Encounters with Deadly Dangers* for the complete story and for additional references and follow-up activities.

ABOUT THIS STORY

Crocodiles are bigger than their cousins, the alligators. The snout of a croc is narrower and more pointed. Crocs are more aggressive, and quicker to attack.

A crocodile may show a crooked smile, but everyone knows that smile can't be trusted. Crocodiles are ambushers, lying in wait, still as a harmless log in the water. Then, *pow!* They pounce. Great jaws slam shut. Another victim is dragged underwater and is gone.

Maybe crocodiles look dangerous to us, even when they are lying quietly in the sun, because they *are* dangerous, as dangerous as any big predator on earth.

The events included in this story represent normal, prototypical behavior for each species mentioned. The actions and events in the story happen many times each year in the wild.

A "Croc" of Jaws

The current of this meandering river in Kenya's Nairobi National Park flowed thick, brown, and lazy past steep banks of sandy dirt, thick clumps of bushes, clusters of acacia and taller sausage trees, and endless fields of waving savanna grasses that were badly trampled at several places where the shallow slope of the bank created a natural watering spot.

The young crocodile was planning his first mammal hunt. He had watched adults attack countless beasts at the watering spot. He was sure he knew the techniques and patterns for an attack. He was tired of fish and hungry to make his first mammal kill.

The young crocodile treaded water among lily pads next to the watering spot, waiting, watching, his eyes and nostrils above water, but hidden by the thick pads. A family of elephants wandered down to drink and bathe. The young croc didn't dare attack even the infant elephant when it stuck its trunk into the river for a drink.

He had watched other crocodiles attack elephants. One was trampled to death by an enraged mother elephant. One was picked up by a bull elephant's trunk, shaken so hard its back snapped, and tossed into the high branches of an acacia tree, where its dead bones bleached snow-white before they fell back to the ground.

The sun set. An orange glow filled the western sky. A group of zebras nervously edged down the gentle slope to the river. Zebras were the perfect target for his first catch!

Two zebras lowered their heads to drink. Others scanned the bushes and grass beyond for signs of predators.

It was time to attack. The young crocodile allowed the current to carry him creeping forward, nearer and nearer, only eyes and nostrils above the water.

In the distance a hyena cried. It was answered by the nearer roar of a lion. All the zebras raised their heads to listen.

Closer ... closer drifted the young crocodile. He could smell the zebras, even hear the buzz of flies that hovered around them.

One mid-sized zebra stood with both front hooves in the water. That one would be the crocodile's first kill.

The zebra gently dropped its head for another drink.

Racing forward on his webbed feet, driving forward with his powerful tail, the crocodile erupted like a deadly torpedo from the quiet river in an explosion of foaming water. His great upper jaw swung open.

He rammed into the zebra, colliding with its soft underbelly just behind its left front leg. He slammed his jaw shut, locking his teeth into the zebra's flank with amazing power and force. Water poured from his mouth as his jaws crashed shut. A cloud of hissing vapor blew from his nostrils like steam from a boiling kettle.

Zebra ribs cracked with a loud snap. Zebra skin was punctured and torn. Zebra blood flowed.

The zebra staggered and bellowed, but did not fall as it might have if attacked by a bigger crocodile.

With all his might the young crocodile threw his body into a violent spin to flip the zebra off its feet and into the water. Splashing water sprayed across the drinking spot. The other zebras fled to the safety of the top of the bank.

But the stricken zebra instinctively spread its legs for better balance. The crocodile's flip didn't work. Though flesh was torn and twisted from its chest, the zebra stayed on its feet.

Ears plastered back against its head, eyes wide and white with terror, the zebra bellowed a cry for help. Then it bucked in a desperate try to throw off the crocodile.

But the young croc's hold was good. His massive jaws locked onto muscle and bone. He flopped and shook as the zebra bucked, but he did not let go.

Now the struggle turned into a desperate tug-of-war. Crocodile claws dug in. His tail thrashed in the shallow water. Again he tried to flip his body and throw the zebra off its feet.

Again the zebra resisted and stayed upright. Its hooves frantically beat and stomped on sand and dirt, pulling away from the deadly river.

The crocodile was losing the contest. Inch by inch he was being dragged out of the river. Though badly wounded with its front leg painted red from flowing blood, the zebra slowly pulled the crocodile toward the sloping bank.

This was not going right. The young croc had never seen a crocodile being dragged away before. Crocodiles were supposed to savagely throw their victims into the stream. Still refusing to let go, the crocodile was suddenly unsure of what he was supposed to do next.

A deep, throaty growl rumbled from a crocodile on the other side of the zebra. There was a great "thud," a deep shudder, and the zebra seemed to lift off the ground and bound sideways toward the young crocodile. An 18-foot monster adult had joined the hunt and had crashed into the zebra, locking onto its other side just in front of the rear leg.

With a yelp of pain and surprise, and a weak bleating call, the zebra's back legs collapsed. It sank onto its haunches.

Now a second adult raced forward to lock onto the zebra's shoulder, just above the young crocodile.

The young crocodile realized there was suddenly great danger here. First, he was on the bottom of a growing pile of massive adult crocodiles and a dying zebra. He could be crushed. Second, he was still small enough to be considered part of the feast by older crocodiles. If he held his grip and his ground, he would more likely *become* dinner than *get* dinner.

Reluctantly, the young crocodile released his hold and scurried back toward the river as one of the adults snapped at his hind leg.

From the safety of a sand bar, the young croc bellowed his protest as three adult crocodiles savored his meal, *his* zebra, *his* first mammal catch.

Again he cried his frustration and rage. He was answered only by the distant roar of a hunting lion.

There were still plenty of fish in the river. He would grow. There would soon come another day and another hunt.

FOR FURTHER READING

Here are a few good books to let you read more about crocodiles.

Brennan, F. *Reptiles*. New York: Macmillan, 1992.

Kelly, L. *Crocodiles: Evolution's Greatest Survivor*. London: Allen & Unwin, 2007.

Perry, P. *The Crocodilians: Reminders of the Age of Dinosaurs*. New York: Franklin Watts, 1997.

Rue, L. *Alligators and Crocodiles: A Portrait of the Animal World*. New York: New Line Books, 2006.

Simon, S. *Crocodiles and Alligators*. New York: Checkmark Books, 1999.

Sloan, C. *Super Croc and Other Prehistoric Crocodiles*. Washington, DC: National Geographic, 2002.

Tibbitts, A., and A. Rooscroft. *Crocodiles*. Mankato, MN: Capstone Press, 1992.

See your librarian for additional titles.

"Lion" Around

A Young Lion Must Fend for Himself after Being Driven from His Birth Pride

This story is extracted with publisher's permission from a story of the same name in Close Encounters with Deadly Dangers (Libraries Unlimited, 1999). See Close Encounters with Deadly Dangers for the complete story and for additional references and follow-up activities.

ABOUT THIS STORY

Lions are often called "kings of the jungle." But lions do not live in jungles. They live in open savanna grasslands dotted with acacia trees. And lions' behavior is almost the opposite of what humans would consider to be noble and "kingly."

Mighty king lions are lazy. They would rather steal food than hunt their own. Male lions are bullies who don't work, don't help raise the young, rarely hunt (leaving that chore to the females), and don't make any real contribution to the lion pride (the name of a lion family unit). They simply muscle in and take whatever they want: the softest grass and best shade during the heat of the day, the tastiest parts of everyone else's catches.

So why do we call lions "kings"? Because they are the biggest predator in their ecosystem. Hyenas, cheetahs, wild dogs, jackals, and leopards hunt and kill as efficiently as lions. However, lions can overpower every one of these other predators on the African plain and steal their food.

But what about a young male lion who has recently been driven out of his birth pride—as every young male lion is? Many of these lone males starve before they learn to hunt. It is the most dangerous and deadly time in a lion's life.

The events included in this story represent normal, prototypical behavior for each species mentioned. The actions and events in the story happen many times each year in the wild.

"Lion" Around

A sizzling red sun-ball eased over the eastern horizon. But only a fuzzy, orange glow reached the ground through a dense layer of fog. Dew clung thick to the grass and soaked the hairs around the young lion's oversized feet as he padded softly across this 10,000-square-mile savanna grassland. He stopped, head raised, listening, smelling, and he roared.

His cry was answered by the threatening roars of a nearby pride, announcing he would not be welcome in their territory.

He lowered his head and trudged on alone. His empty stomach twisted in a painful growl. He had never been this hungry in his young life.

As the fog evaporated around the young lion, he snarled in frustration at two pilot birds hopping through the grass. It had been another bungled night of hunting. Now he faced another day of hunger. Already his skin hung loose around him. His ribs had begun to show through his hide.

Why hadn't he paid more attention when the lionesses jogged out to hunt? Why hadn't he watched his mother and sisters more closely? Why had he always felt compelled to play instead of seriously practice his hunting? Why hadn't someone told him that he'd be driven out of the pride once his mane began to grow?

Again he snarled. What was *wrong* with chasing his own tail? It was fun. So was pouncing on sticks and beetles. He still liked to do it, even though he knew it was juvenile.

The lion shook his mane in bitter frustration. This mane would grow handsomely darker into a chestnut-brown masterpiece as it continued to lengthen and thicken. His body would someday fill out into 450 pounds of muscle to match his now oversized and gangly feet.

He thought back over the failures of this night's hunt, the seventh since he had been driven out to fend for himself. Shortly after complete darkness, when a lion's hunting period was just beginning, he heard the distant triumphant cries of successful lionesses and the angry squabbling of lions over rights to the kill. It made his desperate hunger and loneliness seem overwhelming.

He spotted a lone gazelle—the perfect meal for a lone lion, the perfect chance to prove his hunting prowess.

Lions hunt primarily with their eyes, as do all cats, and secondarily with their excellent hearing. They have a sense of smell almost as good as a tracking dog's, but rarely use it on the hunt.

Instinctively his body dropped into a low crouch as he crept forward, now invisibly blending with the golden grass. His mind flashed through every rule he could remember. Circle downwind. Approach slowly in a low, zigzag pattern. Freeze whenever the prey lifts its head. Don't be distracted by passing birds or mice. Don't roll over to scratch an itch or bat your sister. If only he hadn't turned every hunt into a game, knowing one of the adult lionesses would catch enough to let him eat his fill.

The gazelle paused in its chewing and lifted its head, not in alarm, just in a routine, wary check of its surroundings for signs of danger.

The lion froze. Not a muscle moved. He breathed silently through open mouth, his hot, stale breath bending the grass like a gentle wind. His shoulder muscles burned with the strain of holding his 300-pound body motionless before the gazelle dropped its head back to the grass, content that all was safe.

The lion resumed his quiet creep. For the first time he *felt* like a hunter. *He* was stalking an unaware prey as great lions had for countless centuries. His lips pulled back, baring his deadly teeth. His front claws stretched out to scrape the dirt as he slinked forward.

Closer and closer he crept, his stomach brushing the ground.

Forty yards to go. Thirty yards to go.

He could hardly stand the nerve-wracking tension of his hunt. He wanted to bound forward and announce his terror-inspiring presence with a mighty roar.

He was almost there. He could already feel his claws leaping through the air to sink into the gazelle's shoulder. Lions do not kill with their fierce claws. Those are used to hold onto the prey while the teeth deliver a killing bite, usually breaking the neck.

He could taste the meat and smell the warm blood of his kill. He could …

Again the gazelle glanced up. Too late the lion froze.

He had been spotted when still 25 yards away!

He had been daydreaming instead of concentrating on his hunt. The gazelle bolted.

The lion roared in anger after it.

Why did hunting have to be so hard?

By mid-morning, fed or not, lions settle down to nap through the heat of the day. But the young lion was too hungry to sleep. He aimlessly wandered under the blue sky and fierce tropical sun, panting to cool himself, thinking only of food and the lost comfort of youth.

He spotted a family of warthogs as they emerged from their shallow burrow—a mother and five children. Warthog was hardly the noble meal of a king. But it was better than starving. Swallowing his pride, the lion dropped into a crouch and scurried toward the warthogs.

The desperate lion inched closer to the family as they trotted in line behind their mother, secure in the belief that the heat of the day was adequate protection from the great predator cats of night.

The lion pounced from his concealment with a thunderous roar. The warthogs scattered, squealing in fright. He sprang first after one runty juvenile, then turned to chase a fatter, older victim. But the warthog disappeared down the entrance of a shallow tunnel before the lion could swat it down with his paw.

The lion roared in rage. He couldn't even catch a warthog!

No! He would not go hungry any longer!

Discarding the last of his noble pride, the lion began to dig after his dinner. Sandy savanna dirt sprayed out between his hind legs as his front feet and claws tore away the tunnel's roof.

Five feet, and now six feet, of warthog tunnel lay exposed. The lion was shamelessly covered in dirt. His eye caught a glimpse of flesh through the spraying dirt and grass.

He lunged forward. His claws sank into the flesh of warthog rump. He dragged the squealing prey from its hiding place and delivered the killing bite like an experienced adult.

One front paw resting on his first solo kill, the lion lifted his head and bellowed a triumphant roar that echoed over the noontime plain.

This was *his* world, *his* grassland, *his* kingdom. He *would* survive to be king. He had just proved his right to ascend to the throne. Then, for the pure joy of it, he chased his tail before eating.

FOR FURTHER READING

Here are a few good books to let you read more about the life cycle and behavior of lions.

Anderson, J. *Lions (Wild Ones)*. Minnetonka, MN: Northwood Books for Young Readers, 2006.

Arnold, C. *Lion*. New York: Morrow Junior Books, 1995.

Darling, K. *Lions (Nature Watch)*. Minneapolis, MN: Carolrhoda Books, 2000.

Grace, J. *The Nature of Lions: Social Cats of the Savannah*. Tonawanda, NY: Firefly Books, 2001.

Jobert, B. *Face to Face with Lions*. Washington DC: National Geographic, 2008.

Riley, J. *African Lions*. Minneapolis, MN: Lerner Publications, 2007.

Squire, A. *Lions*. Chicago: Children's Press, 2005.

See your librarian for additional titles.

Feeding Frenzy
Three Boys Face a Stream Teeming with Piranha

This story is extracted with publisher's permission from a story of the same name in *Close Encounters with Deadly Dangers* (Libraries Unlimited, 1999). See *Close Encounters with Deadly Dangers* for the complete story and for additional references and follow-up activities.

ABOUT THIS STORY

We have all heard of piranhas. The word *piranha*, like *shark*, has wormed its way into our common speech as a way to describe a person as dangerous and as someone who feeds off other people and hungrily takes what they want without regard to the damage or injury they cause.

The truth is somewhat different. Piranhas are a small South American freshwater fish. They rarely grow to over a foot long and have round, flat bodies. They actually have small mouths and can only nibble a thimbleful at a time when they eat. But inside those petite mouths, piranha have scalpel-sharp teeth and strong jaws that can easily slice through bone.

During the wet season when rivers flow deep and rich in food, piranha aren't dangerous to anything as large as a human, unless that human is injured and trails blood into the water. During the wet season children regularly swim and play in the rivers where piranha lurk.

But in the South American dry season, it is a different story. Rivers shrink. Piranha become trapped in huge schools of hundreds or even thousands of fish. Food is scarce. During the dry season, beware. For then, all the stories you've heard of vicious piranha attacks are quiet true.

The events included in this story represent normal, prototypical behavior for each species mentioned. The actions and events in the story happen many times each year in the wild.

Feeding Frenzy

Three boys stood at the bank of a thin, meandering tributary of the Orinoco River as it snaked its way deep inside the jungle flood plain of Venezuela, South America. One boy, the youngest, stood back a few feet on a thick root outcropping, intently watching the other two. These two stood at the river's edge, a stream really, no more than 10 feet across. Their dark-brown skin glistened in the splashes of sunlight that shown down along the riverbank. Their straight, black hair flopped over their foreheads and was cut straight around the back, looking like an upside-down bowl stuck on their heads.

The three had been sent out hunting to catch dinner for the family.

The youngest one shuddered and peered down at the dark-green waters sluggishly flowing around thick clumps of floating water plants. "Do you think there are piranhas in there?"

"I'm not afraid of piranha," bragged the second boy. "I even swim with piranha."

"Maybe in the wet season," said the oldest. "But this is the dry season. Food in the river is scarce for the fish."

The older boys lunged toward the youngest. "Maybe we'll throw you in and find out!"

The youngest boy screamed in fright. The older ones laughed.

Then they froze, listening. They heard the crunching and crackling of something walking through the underbrush across the stream. Instinctively, all three crouched low, holding still, watching. Instinctively, the hands of the older boys crept toward their bows.

"There!" hissed one of the older boys. "A capybara."

"If we catch a capybara," said the other, "we'll feed the whole village and be heroes."

Adult capybara, the world's largest rodent, often grow to over 100 pounds and make for a delicious feast.

"How can we catch it?" whispered the youngest boy. "It's on the *other* side of the river."

After a long pause, while they watched the capybara shuffle its way through the dense underbrush near the opposite shore, the first boy said, "We'll have to test the water to see if it's safe."

"How?" asked the youngest.

The first boy gulped. "There's only one to find out. Someone has to stick their finger in the water."

Both older boys turned to the youngest. "Stick your finger down in there."

He shrank back in horror. "No!"

"Don't you want to grow up to be a brave hunter?"

"No."

"I'll do it," huffed the oldest boy. "But then *I* get all the credit for catching the capybara."

"You can have it," whispered the youngest. "I'm not touching that water."

Trembling, the oldest boy inched forward as if the water itself would leap up and grab him. He stopped at the river's edge, staring at the peaceful green surface and its soft reflection of the clear blue sky above.

Shading his eyes he tried to peer past the surface reflection to see what evil terrors lurked just below.

"Go ahead. Stick your finger in the water."

"I will!" he huffed and stretched out one trembling finger, pausing several inches above the water. Then his hand darted forward, brushed the surface for one microsecond, and jerked back. "It's safe," he triumphantly announced.

"That doesn't count. You have to *really* stick the finger down in there."

Face tight with fear, the oldest boy jammed his finger into the water and quickly stirred. The other two boys stared over his shoulder, mouths dropped open.

Then the boy screamed and yanked back his finger. A small, neat chunk had been nipped off the end, and blood already trickled down his wet hand and dripped into the water. The surface boiled as countless piranhas dove and pushed to find the source of the blood.

"Oww! My hand! He bit it off!" wailed the boy, shaking his sore finger.

"It's not a bad bite," said the second boy, holding the oldest one's hand still to examine the wound. "Put pressure on it and it'll stop bleeding in a minute."

"We might as well go home," groused the oldest boy. "The capybara ran off when I yelled."

Then all three boys froze as a great crashing across the stream signaled a wildly running animal. The capybara burst back through the vines and underbrush at a frantic sprint, ears pressed back against its head, eyes wide with fright. Behind it a snarling roar broke like a thunderclap across the stream and rumbled like echoing thunder through the jungle.

"A panther!" whispered the boys as they snatched their bows and dove for cover.

Desperately trying to escape from the panther, the capybara hurled itself off the riverbank, leaping far out over the water. Its legs churned as if to swim through the air to the far side of the stream.

The panther, sleek, black, and pure muscled power, blasted through the shrubs, eyes and long fangs gleaming in the pools of sunlight. One step behind the capybara, the panther leapt like a rippling surge of fury after its prey.

In mid-air the cat's outstretched claws locked onto the capybara's back. Its snarling mouth swept down for a killing bite at the neck as they gracefully arched over the water.

Locked together, both animals crashed into the middle of the river with a great splash that soaked the boys as they watched from their hiding place behind a tree on the near bank. They heard the desperate squeals of the rodent as its head momentarily bobbed back to the surface. They heard the panther's roar of triumph turn into wild cries of rage and pain as it struggled to keep its head above water.

The water boiled into a white, frothing madness around the two animals, sounding like a thousand paddle wheels beating on its surface. Only the angry shrieks of the panther pierced through the dull roar of the piranhas' feeding frenzy.

The boys were too transfixed to blink. They were too startled to breathe. One second, 100 pounds of capybara and 200 pounds of snarling black fury hurtled straight toward them. Next second, both animals were swallowed by a boiling cauldron of death in the river, looking like the bubbling pot of some evil sorcerer.

In under four minutes the water calmed. Capybara and panther skeletons floated on the surface, picked white and clean.

Still staring wide-eyed at the deadly stream, all three boys stumbled, trembling, back toward the safety of their village in awe-filled silence. There would be no more challenge of the mighty piranhas this day.

FOR FURTHER READING

Here are a few good books to let you read more about piranhas and the South American river ecosystem.

Aaseng, A. *Animals Attack! Piranhas*. Chicago: Kidhaven Press, 2005.
Gilliland, J. *River*. New York: Clarion Books, 1993.
Goulding, M. *Floods of Fortune: Ecology and Economy along the Amazon*. New York: Columbia University Press, 1996.

Grossman, S. *Piranhas*. New York: Silver Burdett, 1996.

Landau, E. *Piranhas*. Chicago: Children's Press, 1999.

McAuliffe, E. *Piranhas*. New York: Capstone Press, 1997.

Quinn, J. *Piranhas: Fact and Fiction*. Neptune City, NJ: T.H.F. Publications, 1992.

See your librarian for additional titles.

Tiger Jaws
A Tiger Shark Attacks a Porpoise Family

This story is extracted with publisher's permission from a story of the same name in *Close Encounters with Deadly Dangers* (Libraries Unlimited, 1999). See *Close Encounters with Deadly Dangers* for the complete story and for additional references and follow-up activities.

ABOUT THIS STORY

Many people shudder when they think of sharks. Images from movies like *Jaws* flash through the mind. The images produce a picture of a senseless, brutal killer who attacks silently from the invisible depths of the ocean to maim and destroy.

Sharks appear often in human folklore and mythology. They are god-like in the legends and stories from Hawaii and Polynesia. They appear often as pivotal characters in tales from ancient Greece and Babylon.

There are more than 300 species of sharks that inhabit the world's oceans and seas. Only a dozen of these species are dangerous to man. Only three or four come to mind when we think of "shark." The most famous is the biggest of the man-eaters, the great white shark.

But a human is more likely to survive an encounter with a great white than with a tiger shark. Tiger sharks are a bit smaller than the great white, but are more aggressive and fierce. They are more territorial and more prone to attack for the sake of the attack. There is nothing in the ocean more dangerous than a tiger shark patrolling a reef it has claimed as its own.

The events included in this story represent normal, prototypical behavior for each species mentioned. The actions and events in the story happen many times each year in the wild.

Tiger Jaws

Fearlessly covering as much as 50 miles a day, with the coral reef below, the blazing-white brilliance of the tropical sun above, and spirals of wavering blue curtains all around, a tiger shark has laid claim to a long reef a quarter-mile off the Mexican coast south of Acapulco. More territorial than most sharks, the tiger often lays claim to a reef for the whole winter, becoming a true nomad only in the summer.

Nothing in the sea is more dangerous than this tiger shark as it slowly cruises the reef, sensing minute chemical traces of distant food, "listening" for even the faintest distant erratic vibrations of a fish in trouble.

He is a male tiger shark, 18 feet long and weighing almost one and one-half tons. Besides man, there are only two predators for this shark: giant squid and sperm whales. But neither of these creatures frequents shallow coastal reefs. So the shark hunts with supreme and fearless confidence.

Its broad, blunt snout protrudes above a wide, curved mouth and its rows of sharp, triangular, serrated teeth. Its eyes are wide-set and solid, lifeless black. Its dark-gray skin is more coarse than the roughest sandpaper and can tear the flesh off a human leg just by brushing past.

A faint trace smell, a few molecules of scent in a liter of water, makes the tiger turn left and nose higher along the reef. Its tall tail beats harder, propelling the shark past craggy coral beauty. A shark's long-range sense of smell is as sensitive and accurate as that of any species on earth.

The tiger senses, or feels, splashing vibrations half a mile ahead. Its stomach juices begin to churn. The smell of porpoise wafts strong in the water. The combination of smell and vibrations becomes an unstoppable urge, a calling, an instinctive demand for the shark to eat, to kill, to attack.

Swimming hard, the tiger shark rises to the late afternoon surface of the Pacific. Its slightly curved dorsal fin slices through the calm waters, casting up a small wave like the bow of a boat.

Ahead it senses the presence of a small family of porpoise, flopping, splashing, playing in the water. The tiger circles wide, searching for a pup—always easier to attack than a full-grown adult.

It senses two.

Silently it glides below the surface. The best attacks come with total surprises from below. The tiger shark drifts cautiously closer. A group of adult porpoises can gang up on a shark, battering it with their hard noses, crushing the shark's internal organs.

The tiger circles along the reef, measuring the speed and position of each porpoise with its mid-range electro-receptors. Its lateral lines detect the awkward splashing of a young porpoise trying to leap clear of the water as the adults do so often in their play.

The pup is momentarily unguarded by adults as they romp, unaware of the danger swiftly closing in from below.

Again the pup tries to breach, lifting its tail as it soars into the air.

Thrashing its mighty tail, the tiger sharks drives forward, rushing to meet the pup where it will crash back into the water.

Adults become aware of the charging shark. With squeals and clicks of alarm, they rush to the pup's defense. Though only five feet long, and less than a quarter the shark's size, porpoises are faster, more maneuverable, and fiercely protective.

The pup giddily crashes back into the water, thrilled at its first successful breach. The tiger surges up from below on a beeline to the pup. Adults sprint to form a protective shield around the youth.

Falling down, down into the water column under its downward momentum, the pup hears the squeals of alarm, and pipes out its own shrill cry.

With a final lunge the tiger crashes into the pup. Fearsome jaws lock onto the three-foot pup just ahead of its tail. Teeth grind and slice through tender porpoise hide, flesh, and bone.

The first of the adults, like a screeching rocket, slams into the shark's side at almost 50 miles an hour. The five-foot porpoise is dazed and wallows drunkenly back through the water. The shark is knocked sideways, but maintains its grip on the youth.

With a violent twisting of its great head, the tiger shakes the pup like a dog shaking a bone. Blood flows thick into the water from the terrible gash deepening on the pup's side.

A second adult and now a third slam into the shark's body.

The shark does not feel the pain. It has no nervous system to detect and measure pain. Though the thundering blows from enraged porpoises have shattered rib cartilage and badly bruised several internal organs, the shark has smelled blood and is in a frenzy to feed.

Again the tiger violently shakes the pup in an attempt to kill it. It releases its hold to swallow the first ragged bite it has ripped from the pup's flank.

Simultaneously five adult porpoises crash into the shark's tough hide like racing motorcycles slamming into a stalled pickup truck. Porpoises noses are scraped and bloodied by the shark's rough skin.

Stunned, the shark is rolled backward by the blow. Its tail responds sluggishly as the porpoises have crushed part of its spinal column.

The pup is forgotten. The tiger limps back into the deep along the front wall of the reef. The porpoises huddle around the mortally wounded pup, nursing and reassuring it.

The tiger shark, a magnificent killing machine perfected over countless millennia of evolution, hardly notices its injuries as its thoughts return to the next hunt and its next meal.

FOR FURTHER READING

Here are a few good books to let you read more about tiger and other reef sharks.

Burnham, B. *The Tiger Shark*. New York: PowerKids Press, 2001.
Ellis, R. *Monsters of the Sea*. New York: Alfred Knopf, 1994.

Gourley, C. *Sharks! True Stories and Legends*. Brookfield, CT: Millbrook Press, 1996.

Lawrence, R. *Shark! Nature's Masterpiece*. Shelburne, VT: Chapters Publications, 1994.

Markle, S. *Outside and inside Sharks*. New York: Athenuem Books for Young Readers, 1996.

Michael, S. *Reef Sharks of the World*. Monterey, CA: Challengers Books, 1993.

Murray, J. *Tiger Sharks*. Edwina, MN: Abdo Publishing, 2004.

Perrine, D. *Sharks*. Stillwater, MN: Voyageur Press, 1995.

Welsbacher, A. *Tiger Sharks*. Mankato, MN: Capstone Publishing, 1998.

See your librarian for additional titles.

Index

About the Author

KENDALL HAVEN is a nationally recognized master storyteller and the author of numerous books, including *Marvels of Math, Write Right!* and *Close Encounters with Deadly Dangers*. A former research scientist, he is based in Fulton, California.